CROSSING
THE
ELDE BRIDGE

CROSSING THE ELDE BRIDGE
A MEMOIR OF SURVIVAL

MARIA CLARK & DAVID LAPHAM

Outskirts Press, Inc.
Denver, Colorado

To the innocent victims of injustice and oppression everywhere

Acknowledgements

A very special thanks to Dr. Marvin Newman for his encouragement and support over the years. Without his persistent nudging, this story would never have been told. A huge thank you also goes to Mr. William Clark for his patronage and support.

Words cannot express our gratitude for the efforts of David's Florida Writers Association critique group and fellow writers for the many hours of review, editing, and advice. Thanks a million to Frank Kennedy, Elaine Person, Joyce Sanderson, Minda Stephens, Kari Zamaitis, and Liz and Warren Spahr. Thanks, too, to Deni Senteral-Scott and all the wonderful folks at Outskirts Press.

And finally, last but certainly not least, we wish to thank Sue Lapham, our first reader, harshest critic, and editor extraordinaire.

8/10

Table of Contents

Prologue

The Hungarian winter came early and cold, howling winds whipping the last golden leaves across the endless *puschta*, the vast prairie, while covering the ground with a soft white blanket—the first snow of the season. It is different now, but at the time there were still widely scattered estates owned by aristocrats, dukes and counts, their manors small fiefdoms from another time.

One such estate stood in a wide forest clearing, a not-too-small castle made of massive stones, with a round turret on one side. The many rooms, most with floor-to-ceiling windows and doors, were all large: a warm basement kitchen, always alive with activity; a well-lit music room; a library filled from floor to ceiling with hundreds of books and fine, old, brown leather furniture; luxurious, well-appointed bedrooms on the second floor. From the top floor a winding staircase led to the turret, opening into a cozy room with windows all around providing an unobstructed view of the vast prairie and forest. Under the windows a built-in bench covered with embroidered velvet pillows circled the room. Unseen hands from the hallway outside fed a tall, white-tiled stove, which dominated the room and emitted a crackling warmth. The pungent fragrance of apples baking in a small nook in the back of the stove enveloped the room. It was the favorite haunt of the little girl who lived in the mansion.

Her most cherished moments that winter were when she and her grandmother went up into the turret and sat together on the bench, the child resting against her *oma*. From the toasty warmth of their sanctuary they watched the icicles shimmering in the sunlight and the deer and pheasants at the feeders outside in the bitter cold landscape.

And she listened to her grandmother's many stories. Oma spoke often of her husband, the little girl's grandfather, of the good times they shared before the First World War, and of their experiences during it. World War I had ended in 1918 before the birth of the little girl, so, although she was fascinated by all the stories, she was confused. She had no idea what a *krieg* was. Her grandmother used the word so often. One day as she cuddled in her grandmother's arms she finally asked her, "Oma, what is war?"

The old woman answered with great sadness, "Oh, my child, I hope you never have to find out."

But she did find out. I found out. I was the little girl in that lofty, warm turret and I came to know war and all its horrors. This is my story.

1

Split, Dalmatia

December, 1939. I was a young girl thinking only of Christmas, which was a few days away. Mademoiselle Martín, my French governess, and I were walking through Split, where we were living at the time, and I was bubbling with joy. I loved Christmas, and I loved this place.

Split, nestled on the shores of the Adriatic, is built around the fourth-century palace of the Roman Emperor Diocletian and incorporates the ruins of the palace, including its gates, walls, arches, mausoleums, and temples. I loved the many intimate streets, so narrow they resemble hallways. Split is the perfect place to be in winter.

The day was warm for that time of year. The blue-silver Adriatic shimmered under a bright, cloudless sky. I was wearing a raspberry-colored dress and matching sweater and was feeling very childish and ebullient, skipping around, singing a little French children's song, *"Sur le Pont D'Avignon."*

"Come on, Mademoiselle Martín. Let's dance," I said.

CROSSING THE ELDE BRIDGE

She laughed. "Oh no, no. I can't. My skirt is too tight."

I continued skipping and singing as we crossed the central square of town, the Square of the People, and approached the fancy gift shop on one corner. It was my favorite store in all of Split. In this shop two years before I had seen an expensive, golden crystal vase etched with a white floral design. I didn't receive any allowance as such, but I did get gifts of money from time to time, and I always tried to save it. When I saw that lovely vase, I wanted it badly as a gift for my mother, and I used all the money I had to buy it. When I gave it to Mamá, she burst into tears of happiness.

I stopped momentarily at the gift shop, looking in the window and remembering the beautiful vase and Mamá's joy. Then I skipped on, Mademoiselle Martín following behind me. I was living in a world of peace and love and harmony. I knew nothing of the tragedy unfolding in northern Europe and imagined that the world was a beautiful place. Anyone, if they put their mind to it, could achieve anything. That was what I had been taught. If you are good to people, people will be good to you. Everything was wonderful.

Suddenly, in the midst of this glittering blueness and elation, a large, rough hand enveloped my face. I smelled a sickening odor. I tried to break free, but strong hands grasped me, and I couldn't. I tried to scream, but I couldn't. I remember thinking, Mademoiselle Martín, Mamá. Then everything went black. My fairytale childhood ended at that moment, and the reality of the rest of my life began.

☙ ❧

When consciousness returned, I was groggy and dazed. At

first I thought I was having a nightmare. I was standing in total darkness, pressed in so tightly on all sides that I could hardly move my arms. The air was close and warm, and there was a pervasive odor, not the sharp, strong smell that had overcome me, but a heavy stench.

Then I realized that my eyes were open and I wasn't dreaming. I couldn't move my arms because other people were crushing me all around. People were packed into this space I was in so tightly no one could move. I heard moaning, crying, whimpers. I could barely breathe. The stench filled my nostrils. It was stifling.

I was terrified and began to cry. What had happened to me? Where was I? Why was I here? Where were my parents and my grandmother? Where was Mademoiselle Martín? Yes, this has to be a nightmare, I kept telling myself. I'm going to wake up in my bed, and I'll be snug and warm, and the sun will be shining, and Oma will come in and hold me. Everything will be all right. But as time passed everything wasn't all right. This wasn't a nightmare. It was real.

Exhausted and confused, I passed in and out of consciousness. After an eternity, I awoke to more light. I was tall for my age, and I could see over some of the people around me. At the far end of the space, up high, I could see a small window. The surface I was standing on was moving with a rhythmic clackety clack, clackety clack, and I realized that we were in a railroad car of some kind. Because my family almost always traveled by automobile, I had only ridden on a train once in my life, when I was six, and not in a car like this. The car we had ridden in then was luxurious with velvet seats and windows and lots of room. This car was rough and wretched. I had never in my life been in a place so horrible.

CROSSING THE ELDE BRIDGE

And who were all these people? Where did they come from? From the little that I could see and hear, they seemed to be poorer than I was and many of them were foreigners. Some spoke Croatian or German, but many spoke languages I didn't know. Turkish? Greek? And they smelled as if they were unwashed and had been for a long time, like many of the field workers on my grandmother's estates.

Hours passed as I dozed off and on. At one point, I felt something wet and warm on my leg. An older man stood on my left, crushed against me. He was taller than I, and he never looked at me or said anything. He just stood there with a sad, bewildered expression on his face—and urinated on my leg. I was horrified. I could not believe that anyone would do something like this. Later, my horror at what had happened diminished when I, too, could hold myself no longer and felt my own urine run down my legs. I just stood there in agony, humiliated.

This was the beginning of being diminished, of one's pride being systematically destroyed, of losing the feeling of being human. It was the beginning of "you are nothing." An innocent, young girl, completely traumatized, terrified. And it went on and on. Where was this train going? I was a good, Catholic girl. Where was God to let this happen? There was never an answer.

I have no certain idea how long we were on the train. I do know that the longer we traveled the colder it got. Reflecting back later, I guessed that we were traveling three or four days, and it was probably about a thousand miles. As time went by I could hear my stomach growl, and then I felt awful pangs of hunger. Even worse was the thirst. Although I tried to create saliva to swallow by rolling my tongue around in my mouth, it became so dry that my cheeks felt glued to my teeth. My mouth burned. I tried to think good thoughts, thoughts of my grandmother and me in our little turret room in Hungary, thoughts of Christmases there.

༄

Christmas. Christmas for me was a magical time, my favorite time of year, especially when we were at our estate in Hungary, where we had acres and acres of land, a grand, old house, and stables with all kinds of animals—horses and cows, ducks and geese, and innumerable dogs and cats. And at Christmas there was always snow.

Our house had a huge salon, with a high ceiling and tall French windows covered with damask drapes. The week before Christmas the drapes were closed and the door was locked so that I couldn't get in, because the Kristkind, the Christ Child, was working on the tree and bringing in presents. On Christmas Eve we went to Mass, then all gathered around the locked salon door, family and servants alike. I wore a long dress and recited from memory a poem that my mother had written, a different one every year. Then the doors were thrown open. Oohs and ahs filled the crisp night air. Inside the salon a beautiful silver spruce tree, adorned with hundreds of lighted candles, soared to the ceiling. A long table almost the length of the room was filled with presents for everyone, family, friends, and servants.

As I entered, eyes wide with delight, Oma would say to me, "Look. Look at that window. Can you see? Can you see?"

And, yes, I could always see the gossamer fluttering of the Christ Child's gown as he flew out the window. I was bursting with excitement.

After everyone had opened their presents, Mamá would play

the piano and Tata, my father, would sing "Silent Night." Then we all would put on our coats and march down through the snow to the stables, which had been spotlessly cleaned. There we would feed the livestock to honor the animals in Bethlehem who kept the baby Jesus warm at night. Then we would hurry back to the house for a Christmas Eve dinner of fish, the meal lasting late into the evening. I was exhausted but so wide-awake from the excitement that when I did go to bed I couldn't sleep for a long time. The next day, Christmas Day, we would sleep late and then have another feast of pheasant, beautifully prepared vegetables, salads, and wonderful Viennese pastries.

Unbearable hunger and thirst, the awful stench, and the bodies pressing against me on all sides soon brought me back to reality. Hours, then days went by, periods of complete darkness, periods of muffled light. The train moved along in its rhythmic swaying. Then, it would stop. After a time it would start again. Stop. Start. Stop. Start. And we just stood packed in like cattle, saying nothing to each other.

Finally, the train stopped and did not start up again. Soon the doors of the boxcar opened, and angry male voices shouted, "*Raus! Raus!* Out! Out!" German soldiers. As people poured out the open door, some collapsed and remained lying on the floor of the car. They were dead. I stepped onto the ramp and into the freezing night air. The soldiers had truncheons and beat those who didn't move quickly enough. We were lined up in rows and stood waiting for everyone to get off the train. I was still wearing only my sweater and my damp dress, and I shivered uncontrollably from the cold. I could barely stand.

SPLIT, DALMATIA

When everyone had been herded off the train, we were loaded onto covered trucks and driven to a complex. I learned later that it was the infamous Spandau prison in western Berlin. We were lined up in rows again to stand for what seemed like hours. One by one we were escorted into a long building. I watched as others went in ahead of me, apprehensive because I never saw anyone come out. When it was my turn a soldier guided me into the building, down a short, poorly lit hallway and into a smaller room where there were two or three German soldiers. I guessed by the uniforms that one of them was an officer.

He actually treated me kindly. "Sit down, young lady. What is your name?"

I told him. One of the soldiers wrote everything down. The officer asked me how old I was, where I was from, how I did in school, what I liked to do. I was not allowed to ask any questions in return. Finally, he did ask me what I wanted to be when I grew up.

I had relaxed a bit by then. "Perhaps a great opera singer or a famous author, but what I'd really like to be is a doctor. I want to go to the Congo and treat the natives."

He laughed and chatted with me for several more minutes. When he finished questioning me a soldier took me out and led me to the far end of the building, outside, and into another structure. Another soldier handed me a filthy, thin, brown blanket that was crawling with vermin and led me to a spot midway in the building. There were no lights except from the flashlight the soldier carried, but I could see straw on the floor on either side of the center aisle and bodies covered with blankets like mine. The soldier stopped, shined his light on a spot in the straw, and ordered me to lie down. An old man was already lying on one side of me. Later, another woman lay next to me, but I didn't know until morning, because I collapsed onto the straw, covered myself as best I could and immediately fell into a deep sleep.

✍

"*Raus! Raus!*" Three soldiers awakened us. It was pitch black except for the beams of their flashlights. The soldiers lined us up, marched us outside into the snow and bitter cold—I still had only my sweater and no coat—and instructed us to go to the "toilet," a small, three-sided structure about fifteen or twenty feet long. A wide board with ten or twelve holes in it ran the length of this latrine. We were expected to do our business with other people, men and women, sitting on either side of us and the others from our barracks standing in line right in front of us waiting their turns. No paper. No water or soap. No privacy. Obviously, I had never used a toilet like that. What happened on the train was horrible, but this was worse. I had never seen another person naked. It was totally degrading.

After I finished I stood back in the line and waited for everyone else. Then the guards marched us off to a lighted building, where we got our breakfast. Breakfast consisted of a cup of ersatz coffee, probably made from rutabagas, and two slices of bread, which looked and tasted like sawdust. One slice was spread with a pink gelatin, which was perhaps some kind of marmalade. The other slice had a small amount of margarine scraped on it. We sat on benches at long tables and were not allowed to talk; we would soon learn that we were never allowed to talk to anyone except the guards, and then only when spoken to.

We were given only a few minutes to eat and then loaded onto trucks to be taken to a railway station where we stood on the platform, surrounded by soldiers. People would walk by, spit on us, call us names, but we couldn't say anything, do anything. We were not even allowed to move, to wipe the spittle off our faces. If we did, a soldier would come at us with a bayonet or slap us. Eventually, a train arrived and off we went—to our work house, the Telefunken factory in Berlin.

2

The Work Camp

The Telefunken factory was a four-story, dirty brick building with a service elevator on the outside. I was taken to a large room on the top floor. The windows were painted black and the room looked to be completely sealed. There was neither heat nor ventilation. Dozens and dozens of workstations were lined up in rows. Ether fumes wafted from the far end of the room.

The supervisor, a stern looking woman, showed me to one of the workstations with a strong, glaring light and assigned me the task of inserting six tiny wires, as thin as human hair, into a long glass tube. At one end of the tube was a small hole about half an inch in diameter filled with some kind of goo, and I had to push the thin wires just so through the goo, which eventually hardened. It was very difficult. I had no idea what these tubes were for, but in later years I came to think they were probably radar components.

The glare of the light was so blinding, I had difficulty seeing and inserting the wires. I was already dizzy from hunger and cold. The supervisor told me, "You must finish ten tubes every hour." Sometimes I would look at those wires and they would start swimming and dancing before my eyes. Sometimes I would miss the small hole the wire was supposed to go into, and the wire would bend to the side and break. The German workers, there were a few, wore glasses to protect their eyes from the glare, and they were older and seemed to be experienced. I was the youngest person there, and I, along with the other non-Germans, was not given any kind of eye protection. Every hour the supervisor would come by and scold me for not finishing ten tubes.

In the middle of the first morning she came by and started screaming at me, because I had finished only seven tubes. She grabbed my arm and pulled me away from my work station and into an open space. In the center was something like a gymnastics horse. Two men were standing there. They threw me across the horse, belly-first, pulled up my dress, and started whipping me with short leather whips. I screamed as their whips bit into my legs and bottom. The pain was excruciating. I begged them to stop. Then I fainted. Someone threw cold water in my face and I spluttered awake. The supervisor was standing over me, screaming at me in a harsh voice, "Get up! March! March back to your workstation and let this be a lesson to you." My bottom was bleeding as I tried to see those tiny wires through my tears and sobbing. I don't know how many times that happened to me during my time there.

At noon we got back on the service elevator and went down to a courtyard and across to a cafeteria-like place, under guard, of course. I went through the serving line and was given a cup of water and a potato boiled in its skin with some sort of watery, gray gravy ladled on top. The potato had been frozen and was black with rot. Those first couple of days I said, "I can't eat this," and wouldn't take it. But by the third day I was eating those awful potatoes, rotten or not. Hunger is a strong motivator.

Arbeit macht frei! Work brings freedom! This motto was posted over the gates of Spandau. Work brings freedom. And in Spandau, work we did. Our break for the noonday meal lasted less than fifteen minutes, and we had no other breaks from work during the day—except when we were taken out and beaten. In the late afternoon soldiers came in and once again herded us down to the courtyard, marched us to the train station, and returned us to the prison.

❧

That first day when we returned to Spandau from the Telefunken factory guards lined us up and assigned us jobs at the camp. A lucky few were assigned to work in the kitchen. Others cleaned the latrine. And occasionally, some were assigned to change the straw when it got too filthy with blood, feces, urine, and vomit. When they called my name, I stepped out and a guard led me into our barracks. We walked the length of the building and came to a small hole in the wall, perhaps three feet wide by four feet high. It looked almost like the entrance to a fireplace. The edges were all ragged and uneven as though it had just been broken in with sledge hammers. A strange, putrid odor emanated from the hole. "In there," he pointed. I was terrified. I didn't know what I was supposed to do, but I crawled into the darkness. The room was very small, and straw covered the floor. I couldn't see anything at first, could hardly tell where the walls were, but I heard an awful moaning and a woman mumbling in a language I didn't understand. As my eyes adjusted to the darkness I saw her lying there, her legs spread apart, and I could tell she was in agony. I didn't know why. I thought she might be sick or even dying.

She was in childbirth, and I didn't even know it. Although I did know about menstruation, I knew very little about sex or how babies were born, protected and isolated as I had been. She motioned me forward, and I got on my knees and crawled between her legs. Suddenly, this bloody, slimy blob slithered out of the woman and into my hands. At first, it repelled me. Soon, I realized it was moving and it was a baby. Then I saw this cord attached to the baby and going back into the woman's body. She again motioned to me to hand her the baby, which I did. Then she tore off a piece of her skirt, tied it around the umbilical cord, and bit it in two.

As a child I had set up a small "hospital" in an attic of one of our houses where I cared for birds with broken wings and other small animals with minor injuries, but I had never seen anything like this. I was stunned and nauseous. The woman laid there silently holding her baby, and I moved away toward the opening in the wall.

The guard had been standing right outside the tiny room and stuck his head in. "Come," he ordered, and I crawled out of the room, wiping my bloody hands on the straw and on my dress, relieved to distance myself from that foul stench. I never saw the woman again, nor heard anything more about her. I can only imagine what happened to her and her baby.

Because I had earlier expressed an interest in becoming a doctor and because I had done such a "great" job as a midwife, I was put in charge of the "dispensary." That hole in the wall was the dispensary. I had no medicines and no knowledge as to how to use any if I did, but that was my afternoon job, to care for the sick and dying. I cannot say how many people died in my arms, mostly from dysentery and pneumonia. I remember the old man who clung tightly to me, babbling in a strange language. Then, a rattling came from his chest, he relaxed his grip, and he died. I had never seen anyone die before, but I got my fill of it in those afternoons in the "dispensary."

After our chores in the barracks came supper, which was the same as breakfast, except that, instead of ersatz coffee, they gave us tea, some kind of herbal tea, perhaps chamomile. Of course, we still got the same sawdust-filled bread with the marmalade and margarine scraped on it.

∽∂෨∾

And so the days passed. Emotionally I was numb, completely demoralized. I thought I must be losing my mind, because all this couldn't be true. I would return to normalcy and be with my grandmother and parents. But I didn't. I was sucked down into a maelstrom of anguish. Eventually it got to a point where I thought that when the guards insulted me or beat me, I believed I deserved it. Little by little I was losing my real self. There came a time when I was actually grateful to my tormentors if they didn't hit me too hard.

Physically, I was getting weaker and weaker. The food was not nourishing and hardly enough to sustain life. And because of the strong light and the squinting in order to see the tiny wires I was working with at the Telefunken factory, my eyesight began to deteriorate, and I had a constant headache. I was dizzy from the ether most of the time. Some people fainted from it and had to be taken outside. Once when we were herded across the courtyard for lunch, I ran directly into a pole, because I couldn't see it. Nothing was broken, but I was black and blue for several days, and my head ached worse than ever.

It was bitter cold that winter. Many people were sick, and many died. Once I became very sick and was shaking with fever. But I didn't say anything to anyone, because I knew people who came to the dispensary one day were usually gone the next. One night as I was sleeping I felt something fall across my chest. At first, I didn't know what it was. Then I realized it was the arm of the man sleeping next to me. I wanted to tell him to get his arm off me, but I couldn't, because the three guards walking up and down the center aisle would have beaten me for talking. So I carefully extricated myself and placed the man's arm at his side. When we were awakened the next morning he didn't move; he was dead. As awful as it might sound, death was good in one way. The guards gave the clothes of the dead to us. In that way I got a new dress and a coat.

～◌～

Months went by. Nothing changed. I worked at the Telefunken factory where I was so often beaten. I ran the dispensary in our barracks where people died almost daily. I ate the sawdust-filled bread. I went to the latrine with all those other people. Life was surreal. We couldn't talk. We couldn't move about. We were a group of shadows in a long room with a constant insufferable smell. Women having their periods. Sick people throwing up. People dying. Others relieving themselves where they lay, because they weren't allowed outside. Then, the other shadows, the soldiers, walking up and down all night with their flashlights and rifles. I tried to control everything, my bodily functions and my thoughts, because I really wanted to scream, to get up and run away. Sometimes I heard shots outside. I never knew who was being executed, but I thought a number of times that it would be better to be dead.

This went on and on without my knowing if it would ever end, without knowing why I was there, and without knowing if my parents and grandmother were still alive or where they might be. I sometimes wondered what I had done to deserve this. And, as on the train I asked, where are you, God? Why have you let this happen to me? He never answered.

Winter passed into spring and then summer. One day in August we had just returned from the factory and were lining up before we went to our afternoon jobs. One of the guards called to me, "Come," and I followed him into the building where I had first been interviewed eight months before. The guard escorted me into an office, and I was surprised to see sitting there the same officer who had interviewed me when I first arrived.

He smiled, "Please sit, Maria. I have some good news. The Reich has magnanimously brought your parents and grandmother here to Berlin and has given them an apartment in a very nice section of the city. The government is being kind enough to release you to join them." Then, he looked sternly at me. "However, I must advise you that you are not to discuss your experience here with anyone, anyone. Do you understand?"

"Yes, sir. I understand."

"If we should learn that you have, the consequences will be dire, not only for you but for your parents and grandmother as well. Do you understand?"

"Yes, sir. I do."

"Now, if anyone should ask you why you are here in Berlin, you must tell them that you are here to study medicine. After all, you expressed such an interest, and you've had this experience in our dispensary."

"Yes, sir. I understand. I'm here to study medicine."

"You are an intelligent young woman, Maria. Yes, you are young, but you look much older than your age, and obviously you have had good schooling and upbringing. For its generosity, the government will expect you to use the skills you have to support it. You will be contacted shortly and be assigned work to use your skills. Now, you may go. You will be taken to your parents directly. Good luck, Maria. I know you will do well."

We both stood then. My heart was in my throat. I could not imagine this was ending and that I would see my parents and grandmother. The guard then led me to another room where I was given clean clothes.

After I'd changed he took me outside to a waiting car. A short time later, the driver stopped in front of a large apartment building in Berlin. He got out, opened my door, and told me to go to an apartment on the fifth floor. I hurried up the stairs as fast as I could, although in my weakened condition I stumbled several times. Finally, breathless, I stood at the apartment door and knocked. No one answered. I knocked again. Slowly the door opened and there stood Tata, frozen in disbelief. I fell into his arms, and soon both my parents and my grandmother were smothering me with hugs and kisses. We were all sobbing. After those endless months in hell, I could think of only one thing—I was finally reunited with my family. I was home.

3

Berlin

Home, such as it was. The apartment had a kitchen, bathroom, living room/dining room, and two bedrooms. It was a drab little place, furnished with very basic furniture. Given my upbringing and the opulence of my childhood, I was shocked, even after my months in Spandau. At that time in Germany, uniformity was encouraged. Hitler was trying to take away everyone's individuality, so they would be more dedicated to the Reich. The Volkswagen was the only car produced, and the "People's Observer" was the only newspaper. Food, clothing, gasoline, everything was rationed, everything. Fortunately, my grandmother and parents had been allowed to bring several boxes of personal items with them, and Oma and Mamá had managed to make the apartment at least cozy.

After our tearful and joyous reunion, my grandmother took me to the bathroom for a bath. I thought I was in heaven; the water was so wonderful. I soaked and scrubbed, scrubbed and soaked until the water was cold. Even then, I only reluctantly got out of the tub and dried off. Oma came in with clean clothes. I felt clean on the outside, yet my soul could not forget the filth and stench and horror of that camp. But for now I was safe with my parents and grandmother.

⚮

Over tea and some crackers my grandmother had hoarded we talked, and they told me what had happened. After Mademoiselle Martín and I disappeared, they were distraught and did everything to find me. When Germany had annexed Austria, we had moved to Split, because my parents hated and feared the Nazis so much. But when I was kidnapped they returned to Vienna, hoping to locate me. They even hired a private detective, but to no avail. Mademoiselle Martín and I had disappeared from the face of the earth. We never did hear from Mademoiselle Martín or anything about her. Perhaps the Nazis killed her; I don't know. My parents also appealed to God-knows-how-many authorities and to all their connections. Nothing. The Nazis had completely saturated the Austrian government by then, and nothing my parents or any of their influential friends did helped.

But almost eight months after my disappearance two men in civilian clothes came to our house in Vienna and asked to speak with Oma. They told her that her granddaughter was safe and well taken care of, that she had been taken into custody because she had "expressed herself in a derogatory manner about the great German Reich." A young teenager. Why, I had heard my father and others from many different countries at dinner talking about Hitler and laughing at him. My father referred to him as the "little paperhanger" and said, "Give him enough rope and he'll hang himself." Perhaps someone had overheard his remarks and the Nazis decided to give him a sobering lesson by kidnapping his daughter.

My grandmother owned much property and was well known. By innuendo these men told her that the great German Reich understood family values and would allow us to be reunited if she would be willing to "donate" her assets to the war effort. I was not allowed to return to any of the homes we had, and my parents and grandmother by the largesse of the Nazi government would be transported to Berlin and be given adequate quarters similar to what they were accustomed to. There we would be reunited. And so, Oma signed a document stating that of her own free will and without coercion she would turn over all of her properties and other assets to the German Reich. My grandmother gave up everything she had to save my life, the wonderful Hungarian estate where we so often spent Christmas, the farms in Czechoslovakia, the house in Vienna, the logging operation and saw mill in Croatia, the beautiful villa in Split. In that way, my parents and grandmother came to Berlin.

Their apartment was in a corner building across from Tempelhof Airport. A street and a huge field separated their block from the airport. Quite often hundreds and hundreds of Hitler Youth came to the field marching, singing, and beating drums. Their fanatical ranting made our windows rattle. It was frightening.

The first week after my release, I stayed home with my mother and grandmother. Tata was an engineer and had to work for the Nazis—practically everyone had to work for the Nazis—so he was gone from time to time to Potsdam. But the rest of us stayed home and seldom went out, because, even though we were not Jewish, we were afraid to be seen on the streets and caught doing something wrong.

Mamá and Oma fed me as much as they could. Food even then was scarce. The war was still going well for Germany, but the soldiers doing the fighting were taken care of first. Civilians got anything that was left over. I ate anything I could get my hands on. My grandmother many times would say, "Oh, I don't feel so well today. My stomach is upset." And I would eat what she gave me without thinking. And then I would think, Oma is starving herself just to give me extra food, and I would feel so guilty. Still I ate the food; I was always so hungry.

The second week I was home, a nearby government office summoned me. I, too, would have to work for the Nazis. It was not so far fetched. Even though I was a teenager, I looked older. And, because I had been educated mostly at home by my mother and two governesses, I was more advanced intellectually than most of my peers and spoke several languages. And so, I became an interpreter/translator.

Every day I went to the office and was then sent to various places around Berlin, often with an interrogator or with a set of questions I had to ask people. I would translate for them or just talk with them to gather information. There was never any real interaction with those people though, because to them I was a Nazi. I had been issued an *ausweis*, an identification card with a swastika on it to allow me to travel around the city. And guards were always present, standing there with pistols. Once in a while I could say a pleasant word, but normally I had to be very serious and formal. I still wake up at night wondering what happened to some of those people. Spandau and Plotzensee were not far away.

BERLIN

⁓∂ᘒ⁓

When she was studying at the University of Vienna, my mother had a Jewish friend, Sarah Sagal. They had maintained a close relationship through the years. I remembered "Aunt Sarah" and her husband, "Uncle Heinrich," very well from my childhood. I recall riding once with my mother in her blue Buick through Vienna to visit them. They had a wonderful store, Sagal Coffee. It was very elegant with towering shelves filled with gorgeously decorated boxes of chocolate. Uncle Heinrich carried me in his arms and I said, "That one, please" and one of the clerks got down the box I was pointing to. Then Uncle Heinrich opened it, and I took one chocolate. Then I pointed to another box and another. I had had five or six pieces of chocolate from several boxes before my mother realized what Uncle Heinrich and I were doing and said, "Heinrich, don't do that. She'll get sick." He laughed and replied, "You're just jealous because I'm not carrying you in my arms." Everyone laughed, but, sure enough, on the way home I vomited in Mamá's Buick.

Such were my memories, but after the war had started and my parents had come to Berlin, Mamá and Aunt Sarah had lost contact with each other. Then, by some means, Mamá learned that Sarah was living in the Wilmersdorf area of Berlin and asked me to call on her if I ever got to the area. She could not go herself because she did not have the proper pass. One day I was free, so, armed with my *ausweis*, I walked to Wilmersdorf and found the address. It was in a beautiful old apartment building. At the entrance on the first floor all the names of the residents were engraved on brass plates with doorbell buttons next to each one. Sure enough, there was the name Sagal, listed on the sixth floor.

I rang. Shortly a buzzer sounded, and the front door opened. I climbed the stairs, and there waiting for me stood a young lady in a light blue dress and matching sweater.

"May I help you?" She was very pleasant.

"Excuse me, please, but do you know Frau Sagal, Sarah Sagal?"

"Why, no. No one by that name lives here. I've never heard the name. I'm sorry."

"Well, thank you anyway," I replied and went back down the stairs.

Disappointed, I walked home again and told my mother that Aunt Sarah no longer lived there. Later that night, after we were all in bed, there was a loud pounding on the door. My father got up to answer it. There stood three SA men, Brown Shirts, demanding to speak to me.

"I'm sorry. She's asleep," he replied.

They ordered him to wake me up. Tata got me out of bed, and half asleep in my nightgown I shuffled into the front room.

The three men glared at me. "What connection do you have to the Jews in Berlin?' one of them asked.

"None," I said, puzzled.

He slapped me in the face with the back of his hand. My father rushed forward to defend me, but the other two men stopped him—one jammed a pistol into his neck, and the other held him from behind. My mother and grandmother stood there petrified.

"What connection do you have with the Jews in Berlin?"

I again replied, "None," shaking with fear.

He started punching me, and I fell to the floor. Then he kicked me. I was semi-conscious when they dragged me out to a waiting car and took me to the station for more interrogation. They kept asking me about my connection with the Jews in Berlin, and I continued to say I had no connections to any Jews in Berlin. All the while they continued beating and kicking me.

Finally, they asked, "If you don't know any Jews in Berlin, why were you speaking to a Jewess yesterday afternoon?"

At that time in Berlin the government had a system of *blockleiters*, block captains, who were assigned a certain small area around their homes, apartments, or neighborhoods. *Blockleiters* who reported useful information received some small reward, a pound of sugar, some coffee. Evidently, the young woman I had spoken to the day before was a Jewess. She wasn't wearing the yellow star Jews were required to place on their outer clothing, because she was in her own home. Apparently, a *blockleiter* in the building heard our conversation and reported me.

Just before dawn after several hours of interrogation I was taken back home, severely beaten and with two broken ribs. The SA driver dumped me off at the curb with the admonition that if I ever spoke to a Jew again, I would suffer even more serious consequences, and he hoped I had learned my lesson. We never did discover what happened to the Sagals.

❧❧

Many Nazis horribly mistreated certain people, especially gypsies, Slavic people, (Poles in particular), homosexuals, and, of course, Jews, but they reserved their most venomous behavior for the Jews. I remember going on the streetcar to work one day. It was winter, frigid and snowing. We passed a group of people trying to dig trenches in the frozen ground by the side of the road. They were Jews, their yellow cloth stars pinned to their clothes. Two soldiers with rifles and bayonets stood there guarding them. One man especially drew my interest. He seemed to be older than the rest of the men and women working with him. He wore a fashionable long, black coat with a fur collar and a fur hat. Obviously he was not someone who was used to digging ditches. I watched out of the corner of my eye—you just did not know who might be watching you and who might report you for some small infraction. The man apparently wasn't working hard enough, because a soldier came over to him and smashed him with his rifle. The man fell to the ground, and the soldier kicked him and beat him with the butt of his rifle. As we passed I saw a large red spot growing around him on the ground. I was appalled, but I said nothing.

On another occasion, again in winter, I boarded a streetcar at a square called Innsbruckerplatz. Streetcars had a spacious platform that you stepped on before you went inside the car. Since the car I got on looked crowded inside, I stayed on the platform. At one point a tiny old lady dressed all in black with a long coat and a knitted black shawl boarded the streetcar. She was a Jewess; you could see her yellow star under her shawl. She had a small child with her all bundled up against the cold. The conductor came to collect the fare and he just looked at her yellow star. Then without even blinking he grabbed her and threw her and the child off the moving street car. And what did I do? Nothing.

I recall these instances when I should have done something, but, no, I was young, and I was terrified, just like everyone else. I think of myself as a coward then, but if I had tried to help the man with the fur collar, the tiny old lady, or any other Jew, I would have been beaten or worse.

I do not think people today understand how demoralized

and subjugated everyone was under the Nazis. If you greeted someone on the street and didn't say, *"Heil Hitler,"* you would be punished, so that became the greeting everyone used. You did not even think about it anymore as a symbol of honoring the German Reich. It became just a greeting. *"Guten Morgen"* and *"Guten Tag"* were forbidden. You said, *"Heil Hitler." "Heil."* I never liked Hitler or the Nazis. I feared them, like many others did, I'm sure, and during that period I said *"Heil, Hitler,"* like everyone else.

The Nazis obviously had tight control over society, with severe restrictions over every facet of our lives. In the late thirties and early forties most people had no idea what was really going on concerning the treatment of Jews, only that they were being moved around and harshly treated. Still, there were alarming glimpses.

Once I had to go to the north of Berlin through a section called Wedding. It was a blue-collar area, a not-so-good part of Berlin. In order to get there I took a bus which went up to another station just outside Wedding. There I had to change busses. I had been in that area before, but this time there was a barricade and a big sign forbidding entry.

I had my identification and my *ausweis*, so when I saw a bus ready to leave, I went to it. The guard stopped me, but I showed him my papers. He grumbled something and grudgingly let me climb on. It was totally dark in the bus because all the windows had been painted black. What was this all about, I thought. I sat down in a seat next to the window. The bus was almost empty, and I felt very uncomfortable and ill at ease. Of course, the guard walking up and down the aisle did not help. As we began moving, I noticed that someone had scratched some of the paint off the window, and I could see out a little. When the guard was turned away, I looked out.

Germans are clean and neat people and even in the poorest of circumstances, their houses will be clean and tidy. This area was very rundown and derelict. Disheveled and dirty people seemed to be packed in like ants in an ant hill. It was unbelievably crowded. Garbage was strewn all over. Everyone was just milling around, not seeming to be doing anything. And then I noticed all the yellow stars. They were all Jews. It was horrifying.

I felt so sorry for those suffering people. I did not understand why they had been crowded into this area. And the worst of it was the awful feeling of guilt that I carried, because to them I, with my *ausweis*, was a representative of the Third Reich.

At the time I had no idea that they were being removed, or what was really going on. No one seemed to know about the concentration camps. As time went by more and more rumors and inklings began to surface. Gruesome stories started to leak out, but most people were so petrified, they didn't want to hear and didn't want to believe.

Later, I happened to be at one of the railway stations in Berlin when a train rumbled by. It was a long train of what we would call cattle cars. The train would move forward, stop, move back, stop, and move forward again, apparently adding cars from several different tracks behind it. I couldn't avert my eyes from it, because skeletal hands stuck out and horrible gaunt, sunken-eyed faces peered out through the spaces between the slats. Sickened, I realized those were human beings. I was dismayed, thinking of my own train ride months before. My heart ached for these people.

I never knew if they were Jews or not, whether they were non-Germans, but from what I learned later, I imagine that they were Jews being transported to a concentration camp someplace for extermination. When I told my parents and grandmother what I had seen that day, they became extremely upset and insisted that I must never mention this to anyone.

In this climate of fear my father came home from work one day in a very bad mood. He was distraught and unapproachable. I knew something had happened to him, something really terrible, and I couldn't stop worrying about it. Little did I know. He would not talk to any of us about it. Then, one afternoon he and I went for a walk. It was a brisk autumn day in 1941 and a chill breeze tossed the fallen leaves along the street. We walked for a long time in silence. Something was on Tata's mind and he was deciding how to tell me.

Finally, he said, "Maria, I have a problem, and you must help me solve it. I can't tell your mother or grandmother. It would devastate them. You are the only one I can talk to about this. I know you are young, but you are strong, and you've had a taste of what the Nazis are like. Before I tell you, though, you must promise not to tell a soul, especially not your mother or grandmother."

I was alarmed, but I replied, "Of course, Tata. I promise."

"Well, then, I must tell you that a few days ago, my superior in Potsdam informed me that I must distance myself, legally, from your mother, and of course, you and your grandmother. I must divorce your mother. She and Oma are not German. I have only a little German blood in me and you even less. And none of us are German citizens. Because the three of you are all Slavic, they want to…"repatriate" you, send you back east. I guess I am valuable to them. I cannot, I will not, desert my family, but I don't know what to do. You must help me think of something."

I was stunned. Repatriation. That could mean only one thing. I had visions of those poor people in cattle cars and of Spandau prison. Tata's words crushed me like a death sentence.

He continued, "We can't go anywhere. We can't escape without papers. I just don't know what to do."

I gathered my composure. "Don't worry, Tata. We'll find a solution." The breeze suddenly felt much colder, and I pulled the collar of my coat tighter around my neck.

Nothing more was said, but it was on my mind constantly, and I know it filled Tata's thoughts, too. Weeks went by and his superior said nothing more about it. We both began to hope that the problem might have gone away.

4

Berlin With Love

One day in mid-November, 1941, as I rode to an interview, a young woman climbed on the bus and sat beside me. We exchanged polite greetings. After a few minutes she introduced herself. Her name was Erica Brandt. I introduced myself, and we chatted the whole time we were on the streetcar. I liked her very much, and we became friends.

Shortly after Christmas we were riding together on the streetcar and talking. My favorite subject was food, since I was hungry all the time. Talking about food was rude and impolite, but that's all I could think about. Erica just smiled. She was hungry too.

"You know, Maria, I've been invited to a *Sylvester Abend* party." *Sylvester Abend*, New Year's Eve, was celebrated throughout Central Europe as one of the biggest parties of the year. "A wonderful family who live in Steglitz have invited me and said that I could bring a friend. Would you like to come with me?"

"Oh, my father would never permit it."

She replied, "It will be very nice. They have a beautiful home, and the gentleman is in the food business."

My interest was piqued, and I told her I would ask my father.

"Out of the question," he answered without hesitation.

Even Erica came over and asked. She said that we would go and return together.

"That's very kind of you, Fraulein Brandt, but Maria is much too young."

After she left I pleaded with him. I told him about all the hams and cheeses that I would be able to eat and even offered to sneak some home to them. He was aghast at that. "You're talking like some kind of cheap woman. You don't take food from people's houses." He was very annoyed with me.

Finally, after several days of my pleading, he relented. I know his heart was breaking for me, and I think my mother and grandmother had urged him to let me attend the party. Finally, he agreed that I could go if Erica took me and brought me back— and that I should be home by eleven. I did not care about having to be home by eleven. I was thrilled to be going into a world so different from our dreary little apartment, an elegant home and society more like I was accustomed to as a child. I could not wait for New Year's Eve.

I wore a blue, pleated skirt and a little white knitted top under my only and by now too-small winter coat. It was not eveningwear, but it was my one "good" outfit. Clothes, like food, were strictly rationed. Erica came to get me. The evening was heavenly, cold and crisp, a deep new snow, and a gorgeous moon. We walked and walked. Steglitz was a rather upscale area two or three miles away from our apartment, but it did not seen very far. I was so excited.

We finally arrived at an elegant, old apartment building on the corner of two tree-lined streets. As we climbed the steps, I became very nervous. After the work camp and then living the way I had lived since coming to Germany, I had lost my self-confidence. I thought that I would have to be very careful with everything I said and did, because if these people were real Nazis, then I might get careless and say the wrong thing. I began thinking I should not have come. I should have stayed home. We got to the entry and rang the bell. The door opened and Mr. and Mrs. Erwin Kohler, the owners, escorted us into an exquisitely furnished apartment.

Both Kohlers came from an area northwest of Berlin. Mr. Kohler had come penniless to Berlin. Wanting to be a teacher but without money, he had found a job in a grocery. Mrs. Kohler was a farm girl from the little town of Laaslich to the northwest about halfway to Hamburg. She had left to become an older lady's companion in Berlin. She and Erwin had met, married, and through hard work had eventually become successful in the grocery business themselves. I learned all of this much later, of course. When we met them at the door, Mrs. Kohler seemed a bit stern but very nice. Mr. Kohler, a very thin man, was sweet and kind. I was no longer afraid about being there.

The Kohlers' home was typical of old-fashioned, upper-class apartments of the time with a lovely foyer, a long hallway, and doors off the hallway opening to the various rooms. Beautiful paintings hung on the walls. There were two or three rooms connected by heavy oak pocket doors, and as we entered the first thing I saw was a long table filled with food! I would have liked to have thrown myself at it, but I remembered my manners.

CROSSING THE ELDE BRIDGE

I began to feel much better after having something in my stomach. Everything was fine. Music played on a gramophone. People were dancing and talking in small groups. Erica drifted off, but I stayed close to the food table without being too conspicuous. As I was stuffing a piece of ham into my mouth, a tall, very handsome young man strode up and stood next to me, smiling. He appeared to be several older than I and was wearing a dark gray suit, white shirt, and tie. I'll never forget how handsome he looked. He introduced himself as Jurgen Kohler, the son of the host and hostess. I felt very flattered. I had spent very little time with boys, especially in social situations, and had never had a boyfriend and very few male acquaintances my own age. And here was this handsome grown man paying attention to me.

We talked and danced, and it was wonderful to have my head resting against that dark suit and to inhale the fragrance of the cologne he was wearing. Suddenly, I was in a different place. Jurgen was fascinating, asking me questions and telling me all about himself. He was an officer in the Luftwaffe, a pilot. I stiffened when he mentioned that, but relaxed as he continued to charm me. I told him something of my life. I said nothing about my imprisonment. In fact, I never, ever told him about that. This went on and on, and we were completely absorbed in each other, when I happened to look at a clock on the wall. It was past midnight. My father was going to kill me. As a child I had been free-spirited and had done things I shouldn't have, but I had never disobeyed my parents, had never betrayed their trust.

In a panic, I looked around for Erica and told Jurgen that I had to go, that I was supposed to be home by eleven. "Well," he said, "don't worry. I'll get you home and I'll speak to your father. Everything will be fine."

I thought, great. This will be okay, because he is a very nice looking, very serious, and very impressive young man. Tata will surely understand. I found Erica and told her Jurgen was taking me home. We started walking through the moonlit night, through the crisp, crunching snow. As we crossed a bridge, Jurgen stopped and kissed me. Time stopped. I was in heaven. Nothing mattered. It was the first time I had felt like that in my young life. And he told me that he loved me, and I was enthralled.

When we reached our apartment, he kissed me again before we climbed the stairs and rang the doorbell. My father opened the door and Jurgen started to say something. My father pulled me in and said, "I have nothing to say to you, sir," slamming the door.

Then Tata glared at me. He was livid. "You are showing that you have absolutely no character. An agreement is an agreement. A promise is a promise. I am so disappointed in you. How can I ever trust you again?" I was crushed. Moments before I was in heaven in the arms of this beautiful man, and now I had been cast into outer darkness.

I went to bed and I did not even dare to cry, because my grandmother was sitting there shaking her head. She simply said, "You should have come home when you were supposed to." I think she understood but couldn't say anything else. "Go to sleep. We'll talk tomorrow."

❦

The next day at mid-morning there was a knock on the door. My father opened it and there stood Jurgen. He asked to speak to my father. Tata said, "I really don't want to talk to you. I have nothing to say."

But Jurgen persisted. "Look," he said. "It really wasn't your daughter's fault. There were so many people at my parents' party last night and so much going on, the time just slipped by for everyone. You know how it is at an affair like that. Everyone is having a good time, and even with the best of intentions it's hard to keep track of the clock." He went on to explain the situation and to tell my father how impressed he was with me. When he left Tata had softened considerably.

Perhaps, too, he was thinking of his courtship of my mother. He was a bright, young engineer and well-to-do in his own right, but he was a commoner. Aristocrats did not marry commoners in those days, and my grandmother thought he was just after her money when he came calling on her daughter, my mother. He persevered, and finally Oma gave her permission and blessing. "But I want you to know one thing; she has the clothes she wears and nothing more. That is all she owns. Everything else is mine, and I intend to keep it." Mildly affronted, Tata rose and replied, "Madam, I came to ask for your daughter's hand, not your wealth." Oma and Tata later became the close friends and allies. Jurgen, I suppose, reminded Tata of himself in some way.

Jurgen returned the next day and the next and the next. My father finally realized that he was a good man with honorable intentions, and we were allowed to see each other. I was soon madly in love with him, but in the back of my mind the cloud of deportation settled ominously. I'm sure my father was thinking of it also. Several weeks later, Jurgen asked me to marry him, and I said yes. Normally my parents would never have permitted such a thing at my age, but under the circumstances... I don't know if they argued about it or, if they did, what arguments my father used with my mother and grandmother. I only know that after many days of private discussions they gave us their blessing.

Now I was engaged to a German officer and the threat of deportation ceased to hang over us. Also, the government office I worked for seemed to treat me differently, even when Jurgen was not around, which he often wasn't. Shortly after we were engaged, he left to return to the Eastern Front.

❧

Jurgen's mother, Mariechen, was not happy with our engagement. She had already picked out a young woman she wanted him to marry, and she was very upset that he had become engaged to this "child," this aristocratic Slav who did not even know how to cook or do anything a wife was supposed to be able to do. Once when we were at the Kohlers' home, Jurgen was telling his mother how well educated I was. His mother just pointed at me as if I were not there and said, "She can never be a homemaker. She doesn't even know how to clean a suit for her husband."

"Of course, she does," he replied. "She knows that you scrub stains with naphtha. Right, Maria?" I smiled and shook my head yes. Mariechen just crossed her arms, looked at me, and grumbled.

I did know a few things. As a child I didn't do many "girl" things. I played doctor. I played theater. I played veterinarian. I never played mommy. So, when I was ten or eleven, I suppose, Oma decided that I needed to learn some "domesticity" and made me start cleaning some of the rooms in the house. I threw a tantrum, but she drilled me into quiet submission with her steely eyes and asked, "How can you tell servants to do something unless you know how to do it yourself? How can you supervise their work if you don't know how it is to be done?" In that way she made me clean and dust. The first time I wasn't happy about having to do it and was quite cursory in my dusting. When I had finished, Oma checked my work and made me do it again, scolding me harshly for good measure. So I did know how to clean a house, but I wasn't going to argue with Frau Kohler.

She was right about one thing; I didn't know how to cook. Oma jealously guarded that responsibility. Although we always had at least two chefs with a large staff, she ran the kitchen with an iron hand. To appease Mariechen I agreed to attend a homemakers' school in Berlin, the Lette House, where all young ladies of good breeding went to learn how to be good homemakers. The school was very interesting, and I did learn a lot. I had a lot to learn. The school was good for me, and I have become quite a good cook. Attending the school improved my relationship with Mariechen immensely. I learned many years later from reading her diary after her death that she admired my spunk and willingness to do whatever I had to, in order to become a good wife for Jurgen.

From the very first Jurgen was always talking about the family farm in Laaslich, northwest of Berlin. His mother had grown up on the farm that her brother, Jurgen's uncle, Otto, now ran. Jurgen had spent most of his school holidays there, because he had loved it so much. And so, in late spring when he returned again on leave from his military duties, he took me to Laaslich to meet his aunt, uncle, and cousins. We were formally invited so that they could meet his bride-to-be.

On Saturday morning Oma, Tata, Mamá, Mariechen, Jurgen, and I piled onto the train, which was still running then, and traveled the short distance to Derghentin. Uncle Otto was waiting for us with two handsome carriages, not much different from the carriages we had at the estate in Hungary. It was all surreal for me.

I was very nervous and, yes, even a little afraid. Although Uncle Otto appeared to be stern and gruff, I saw that he was a nice man, and I was soon at ease. I had never been in the countryside of northern Germany, so I spent most of the carriage ride to the farm looking about. The land was quite flat, not much different than Hungary. The little roads were lined with trees, and everything was green, green, green. I immediately came to love this part of Germany called the Prignitz. It was so beautiful. I later learned to love it even more because of the people I came to know there.

That day I was expecting to see an estate like our baronial mansion in Hungary with its stately façade and turret. When we finally arrived, I was surprised and a little disappointed. The place was very primitive. Standing there in front of the old, sprawling farm house was Uncle Otto's wife, Tante Grete, their sons, Wilhelm and Friedrich, and Jurgen's grandmother, all smiling and waving. They greeted us with warm enthusiasm. I immediately felt a part of this family, and Wilhelm, Willy, their youngest son who was my age, and I became fast friends. His grandmother, a little old lady, older than my Oma, always wearing a black dress with her hair pulled back in a tight bun, later became a close friend and supporter.

After formal introductions, the older people sat down to talk, and Jurgen, Willy, and Friedrich took me off to show me the farm. It wasn't Hungary, but it was a wonderful place, which had been in the family many generations. The Kohlers' farmhouse was located across from the church. Several other farms were scattered up and down the road on either side. The Kohler house was old but well-kept and comfortable with many rooms which had been added over the years. As was the custom in that part of Germany, a separate wing had long ago been added, the *altenteil*, where grandparents lived. Otto's widowed mother, Jurgen's oma, resided there.

Behind the house to the left was the machine shed, although the government had long since confiscated all the vehicles and machinery. A washhouse, chicken coop, and outhouse were on the right. A very large barnyard filled the space directly behind the house with a huge, old barn in the back. A large garden with all kinds of vegetables and even grapes lay behind the barn. Beyond the garden green fields of asparagus, rutabagas, potatoes, and waving wheat stretched as far as I could see. I was saddened to know that the Kohlers could not enjoy the fruits of their labor; most of the produce from the garden and fields went to the war effort and was closely monitored by government authorities. Oak, elm, linden, and cherry trees shaded the house and outbuildings and lined all the roads. As I stood with Jurgen and his cousins in the bright sunshine looking out on the endless fields, I breathed deeply to inhale the smell of earth and grass and clean air. No, it was not Hungary, but it was a wonderful place.

We returned to the house for lunch to find all the adults getting along famously. Much to my relief, Tante Grete was taken with my mother. They and Jurgen's mother and grandmother were bustling around setting the meal out, talking, and laughing. Uncle Otto was showing Oma and Tata around the outbuildings. With her experience running her own estates, Oma was holding her own with Uncle Otto and I knew my father could discuss machinery intelligently. They all seemed comfortable with each other. I was happy to see our two families getting along so well.

When we finally left to catch the train in Derghentin back to Berlin, it was almost dark. As we rode along a deer jumped out in front of us and ran across the road. Uncle Otto laughed and said, "I'll have to shoot some of those. I'll bring venison to your wedding." I smiled to myself. I had been accepted into this family.

Shortly after our visit to Laaslich, Jurgen went back to his unit, and I came down with diphtheria. The doctor put me into a clinic that had been converted from a school in Berlin. I was in a room with two men. One was very old. The authorities allowed my mother one visit which lasted only a few minutes. Childhood illnesses had weakened my heart, and I did not handle diphtheria very well. I struggled for breath constantly. One day was especially bad, and I was gasping for air when the old man in my room finally jumped out of bed, ran down the hall, and started cursing at the doctors and nurses to do something for me. "This is a scandal," he screamed. "This girl is dying, and you're doing nothing for her." Finally, a doctor came down and gave me an injection of some kind that probably saved me. Not long after, Jurgen returned home and had me moved to a hospital.

When the hospital released me a few weeks later, I was as weak as a kitten, and, of course, my heart had been affected again. My grandmother came to get me and, because the army had confiscated all of the vehicles, we had to walk. I was so weak, I had to stop every few steps and sit on the sidewalk. When we got to the apartment, I could not get up the stairs, so my grandmother, this little old lady half my size, put me on her back and carried me up. I don't know how she did it, but as she always taught me: "Don't ever think the word 'can't.' 'Cannot' does not exist in your vocabulary."

I did recover, and finally in December of 1942 Jurgen and I were married. It was a grand wedding. My mother-in-law made my wedding dress. Because of the restrictions and rationing, you could buy hardly anything, but in that society, just like any other, you could bribe people, and food was the best currency. So Mariechen was able to obtain the material for my dress. I have no idea how much cheese and sausage that material cost.

We were married at the city hall in Schoeneberg, since people did not marry in churches during those years. A white carriage pulled by two white horses picked me up and took me to the city hall. Two little neighbor girls all in white attended me. After the ceremony we left the city hall and passed through two rows of Jurgen's Luftwaffe friends, all in uniform with crossed sabers.

Walking on the arm of a German officer and passing between two rows of German officers with their sabers drawn and crossed above me was a bit ironic, but I was so happy. For one thing, I was now the wife of a German soldier and, therefore, a German citizen, which meant that my mother, grandmother, and I would not be deported. Even more important, I loved this man very much.

The reception afterwards at the Kohlers' home was a grand affair, a sumptuous feast, thanks to Erwin and to Uncle Otto, who, true to his word, brought venison and white asparagus. We held our banquet at a massive U-shaped table in the same room where Jurgen and I had first met, and we danced and sang and ate until late into the evening.

Jurgen's being an officer in the German Luftwaffe did not bother me all that much. He was actually anti-Nazi, as was his father. Of course, they could not say anything openly. They had to hide the fact, but Erwin always said in private that the best time ever in Germany was under the Kaiser. If only the Kaiser were still around, everything would be all right.

Under the circumstances then, a honeymoon was out of the question, so after the wedding Jurgen and I moved in with the Kohlers. We had a corner room with a fold-out sofa for a bed. Within three weeks Jurgen was gone again, back to the Eastern Front where the war was going badly for Germany.

It was strange for me, and I had a lot of adjusting to do, especially with Mariechen, who was a very practical woman. Erwin was a dreamer, almost a poet, but his wife had her feet on the ground. She kept the books for their business and made pickled beets for the store in the bath tub. She knew exactly how much sugar there was, as well as everything else. She was very precise in all that she did. Still, they were both very kind to me and I did my best to please them. I quickly learned to be comfortable with both Erwin and Mariechen and started calling them the familiar names of *Mutti* and *Vati*, Mom and Dad.

5

Berlin On Fire

I enjoyed those first few months of 1943, living with the Kohlers, getting a little more to eat, not traipsing all over Berlin working. Mariechen was very patient with me, working hard herself but not expecting more from me than I could handle. As I said, I did my best to please her. I helped around the house, cleaning and cooking, doing whatever she asked of me. Of course, I kept our own room, Jurgen's and mine, spotless. But I had leisure time. I missed my husband, but I had many chances to see my parents and grandmother, which I did three or four times a week. That winter was cold, but I enjoyed the walk over to Friednau and back. I was even able to put those eight months in the work camp out of my mind—most of the time.

The relative peace and serenity of my life ended in late Spring, however, when the Allies started bombing Berlin more regularly. At first, they raided only at night. Soon, they were bombing at any hour.

Because of the British attacks in 1940 Berliners had prepared for these bombings. They had dug trenches everywhere. The law required that all buildings had to be blacked out. Cellars were reinforced and turned into bomb shelters. Segments of cellar walls between buildings were replaced with thinner barriers that would still withstand some pressure but could be knocked down with a sledgehammer. That way if the one building was hit, the occupants in the cellar could move over to the bomb shelter in the next building. The government also mandated that each bomb shelter have a certain amount of water, a box of sand to extinguish fires from the Allies' incendiary bombs, first aid equipment, and blankets. Quite a bit of thought had been given to guarding the population against the inevitable bombings.

But no one had any idea of the awesome, ghastly power the Allies could unleash to overwhelm us. When the air raid sirens sounded, everyone raced to the cellars and sat huddled together. First, we would hear the drone of the planes, so many of them; we could hear them even in the bomb shelters. Then came the sickening pounding of the bombs. The buildings and ground shook. Dust filled the air. And all we could do was sit cramped together cringing in terror.

When the bombing finally stopped, most people just sat, shaking, unable to speak, unable to move, but soon children would start screaming, many would become hysterical. It was a nightmare sitting there hardly able to breathe or see through the thick dust, listening to people scream. And when the adrenalin subsided, we experienced the euphoria of still being alive.

This went on for weeks, then months. The smoke and dust were so thick, I often could not tell day from night. As more and more buildings were destroyed, remaining bomb shelters became more and more crowded. Streets and blocks and whole sections of the city were pulverized into unrecognizable piles of rubble. Thousands of people died in the bombings, buried under millions of tons of debris. And the stench of all those rotting corpses underneath the rubble was unbearable. As time passed and the bombings increased in frequency and intensity, water mains were broken, and water became contaminated.

I would have gone insane had not Jurgen been there. He returned to Berlin in early March, because he was having medical problems. We suffered the bombings together. He was my only link to sanity, but he left again in April. The bombings continued, but I had adjusted somewhat. Perhaps he had given me some of his strength. I also discovered shortly after that I was pregnant.

I still managed to visit with my parents, and was with them several times during the bombings. Being so near Tempelhof airport, their area was especially hard hit. I was with them once during a bombing after the Allies started using incendiary phosphorus bombs. Phosphorus explodes into thousands of tiny pieces, and if it hits you it sticks to your skin and burns until it has burned up and you with it.

During one particular bombing, my parents' building was hit. It wasn't destroyed but did suffer some damage. When the bombing stopped, I went up with my father and several of the men to check the damage before those in the bomb shelter came out. Tata and I cautiously climbed the stairs to the fifth floor and entered the apartment. It had been hit but was not destroyed. The whole area was in shambles, though. I was in front of Tata, walking with care. Although the floor looked sound, we had no idea if it was or not. I went into Tata and Mamá's bedroom and there on the bed lay a small bomblet. For a second I froze and then gingerly picked it up and in one motion, threw it out the broken window. It exploded harmlessly when it hit the ground below. My heart was in my throat. I was shaking when my father entered and held me.

Several weeks later I was with my parents when they were bombed out. I remember two things very vividly from that bombing. We had incredible rationing during the war. For example, we were allowed only two eggs per person per year, one for Christmas and one for Easter. My grandmother decided that we would save most of the eggs and not eat all of them right away; we would share only one at a time and save the others in case someone got sick and needed extra nourishment. She put the eggs in a jar and lined it with some sort of orange colored paper. We also received fifty grams of coffee that she stored with the eggs in the bomb shelter, the safest place in the building.

On that day bombs were hitting very close, and when one actually hit our building, we all scrambled into the shelter next door. A good thing, too, because another bomb soon came right through the roof of my parents' building and all the way to the cellar without exploding. After the raid was over we went back into our own bomb shelter to see what had happened. Even though the bomb had not exploded, the containers with the eggs and coffee were both destroyed. I almost cried to see those wonderful eggs mixed with broken glass and dirt. Those damned Americans with their bombs.

Again my father and I went up to assess the damage. My father had a parakeet named Putzi, a pretty, green thing with a bright yellow beak. He was very smart and craved attention. When Tata read the paper, Putzi would sit on the top, watch Tata's eyes, and chatter. Tata would ignore him. And then this little bird would somehow see where Tata was looking, would slide down the page, and would stop on top of that story. We always laughed at that, because he knew how to get my father's attention.

We were never allowed to take the bird down into the cellar when the air raid sirens sounded, so we left him up in the apartment in the bathroom where he was kept at night. Every night Tata would put a board across the bathtub with the birdcage on top and a towel over that.

So, as we carefully climbed up the partially destroyed stairs to the fifth floor, I was thinking about Putzi. When we got to their apartment all that remained of the floor was a tiny bit around the edges of the walls and some of the main beams. The door was blown off and the roof and everything else was gone. I worked my way around the edges along the walls and made it to the bathroom, which had the tile floor still in place.

Putzi's cage still sat on the board across the bathtub, and my heart leapt into my throat. I thought, he's still alive! I was so happy because that little bird meant so much to my father and had brought so much joy into the shabby dreariness in which we had been living. I reached out to pull the towel off his cage—and it disintegrated into dust in the tub. And when I reached in to touch Putzi, he too fell apart in the bottom of his cage. The heat had killed him.

My parents and grandmother lost everything in that air raid, so the government moved them to a school. Later they were bombed out again but were finally allowed to move in with the Kohlers.

⌒◌⌒

CROSSING THE ELDE BRIDGE

In July Jurgen returned once more from the Eastern Front. I was so happy to have him home, because the bombings had gotten much worse. Somehow I felt safe in his arms down in the bomb shelter, even though I knew that was an illusion.

But one day, during broad daylight, the air raid sirens sounded and we rushed down to the bomb shelter. Soon we could hear the planes overhead. Then the bombs started falling. I was terrified and clung tightly to Jurgen. At one point I thought the whole building was going to topple down upon us. We were actually bounced from the ground where we were cowering. And the bombs just kept falling and falling.

Finally, there was silence, a dead, eerie silence. No bombs. No one said anything. Then people started to cough and mumble. Children began screaming. Jurgen and I scrambled to our feet and raced out of the bomb shelter and into the street. The other wing of the building had been hit by a bomb and was burning.

An elderly couple, a brother and sister, lived on the third floor. They had not been in the shelter during the bombing, so we went back into the building and ran up the stairs, with several men following. When we arrived at their door, we could hear their piano and her voice. He was playing the piano, and she was singing! We knocked on the door. The music continued. We banged harder to be heard above the music and the roar of the fires outside. Still they ignored us. Two of the men smashed the door down, and we rushed in. There they stood, the old man and his sister, completely oblivious of us and the fire that was quickly engulfing the apartment from above.

They were intelligent people and knew what was happening. I suppose they had just chosen to bring a little happiness to what they thought were the last moments of their lives. The windows hadn't been broken and were closed. Smoke rapidly filled the room. I hurled a chair through one of the windows, so that we could get some air. Others struggled with the old man and woman, who were protesting. They did not want to leave. Finally, someone grabbed them and carried them down the stairs. Jurgen and I followed, and just in time, because the ceiling began falling in, and we could see the flames.

Jurgen led me down the stairs, and when we came down to the entry hall, the top of the doorframe fell down in front of him. As he tried to kick the flaming wood out of the way, he accidentally kicked me, but we managed to leap through the flames and sprint it to safety.

Pandemonium reined outside. People were running everywhere and screaming. The Allies had used incendiary bombs, and the whole world seemed to be on fire. The roar of the blaze was deafening. The first thing I saw was what we called a "Christmas tree." It was some kind of flare or marker the Allies dropped from reconnaissance planes to mark the area to be bombed, and it was shaped like a Christmas tree. On the opposite corner, part of the body of an Allied pilot, who apparently had been shot down the previous night, hung from the crotch of a tree. Women and old men were throwing whatever they could at those pieces of human flesh hanging down, because that was the enemy who was causing so much suffering. And I remember standing there thinking, dear God, when the world finds out about this there will never be another war.

A bomb had hit the building opposite the Kohlers', and a portion of the front wall had split. Two stories up a small child, perhaps three or four, was wedged down in the split, screaming in pain and terror. We could do nothing but watch in horror. The

CROSSING THE ELDE BRIDGE

flames soon silenced him. And then a man covered with burn-ing phosphorus came running up the street screaming. Two men pushed him into the doorway of a burning building, and he, too, was silent. I think about what can happen to otherwise compas-sionate human beings under circumstances of this nature. What we become. That man, I'm sure, died quickly and mercifully. I did not know who he was, nor the child either, but they will haunt me for the rest of my days.

A few days later, my parents and the Kohlers had a discus-sion. The next day Mariechen and I left Berlin and went to the family farm in Laaslich.

6

On The Farm

Laaslich was heaven. Its one street, its quaint little church, its spacious community meeting center, and its surrounding farms were so quiet and peaceful compared to Berlin. Mariechen and I moved into the *altenteil* with Grandmother. We were a bit crowded, but we had a shelter over our heads and there were no bombs.

Everyone was very kind to me. Grandmother, who was in her eighties, always tried to keep my spirits up, and Tante Grete went out of her way to make me feel a part of the family. They both loved Jurgen very much. He was a favorite grandson and nephew, and both women treated me much the same way they would have treated him. As his young, pregnant wife, I was special in the Kohlers' household.

Uncle Otto was an enigma. From all that Jurgen had told me about the man and from our short acquaintance at our first meeting and the wedding, I knew him to be kind and even jolly at times. He was one of the wealthier farmers in the area and had been selected as some sort of local leader by the Reich. Of course, he was also a member of the Nazi Party, as almost everyone was required to be. You simply did not have a choice about that. But as a local leader in charge of agricultural production, he was under a great deal of pressure.

In the beginning of the war, the plan had been to leave at least one man on each farm to do the heavy work, but as the Eastern Front began to collapse, every able-bodied man, young and old, was taken into the army. That left only women, old men, and young boys to work the farms. Production suffered greatly. And yet production quotas remained high and even increased as months went by.

Uncle Otto's office was between the main house and the *altenteil*, and many times I heard angry shouting when inspectors came around and went behind closed doors. Because of this pressure, I think, Uncle Otto was often brusque and ill-tempered, especially with the workers but sometimes with us, too.

Yet he could be very pleasant. On Sunday afternoons we all would sit in the parlor, where he would play the accordion or harmonica, and I would sing. We would laugh and have a wonderful time, a short respite from the work and cares of the rest of the week.

❧

Life in the country was hard and monotonous. With so few men available, the government shipped in many Poles, mostly women, to help on the farms. Uncle Otto had quite a number of them. They all slept crowded in the barn. Because there were no draft animals and little machinery, the work was backbreaking, especially in the asparagus fields. The white asparagus had to be harvested by hand with a special knife. The dirt around each was scraped away and the curved knife was then inserted to cut the asparagus. The women worked on hands and knees in a line, harvesting the rows, placing the cut asparagus in baskets. They also pulled plows and cultivators like draft horses. Uncle Otto spent much of his time in the fields keeping these women, who were always half starving and on the edge of exhaustion, working.

Not everyone had Poles. Karin Huber lived three doors down from the Kohlers and ran her small farm by herself. Her husband had gone early to the war and had fallen quickly in Russia. Now she was all alone. She was amazing, a very German-looking woman, strong and stout, her blond hair pulled back in braids. She was sweet and gentle, always smiling. Karin not only pulled her own plow and worked her fields by herself, but also kept a clean house and cooked as well. She taught me to bake pound cakes, which were always wonderful. I do not know how she did everything.

She did not have any Polish workers, but at one point she was given a Romanian girl. The girl was a well-educated city-dweller, not much older than I; she had never lived in the country. The Nazis had taken her to work in a *lebensborn*, great buildings where Aryan-looking women were placed to mate with SS troops to produce children for the Reich. When she could not conceive, she was sent to a brothel for officers. There she suffered a nervous breakdown and was moved into the category of field worker. When she was given to Karin to work on her farm, her whole history was publicized, and none of the women in Laaslich would go near her. I guess they thought she had all kinds of diseases and God knows what, and how could she do such a thing? I felt sorry for her. What happened to her was not her fault. There she was, and she couldn't do any heavy work—she could not plow, she did not know anything about farming. Eventually she disappeared. I do not know if she ran away or if the authorities took her, but she was gone, and no one ever heard from her again.

❧

Even in the country, food was still everyone's primary concern. The Prignitz was an agricultural area, and the farmers there were a hearty people from a mostly Slavic background. The Slavic people who settled the area brought with them and kept many of their old cultural traditions, one of them their joy in food. Farming in colder climates required a lot of energy, and it was not uncommon for a farmer to eat a huge breakfast of ham, eggs, sausage, bread, cheese, coffee, and even a little glass of schnapps and then go out into the cold and do whatever had to be done.

And the people of the Prignitz played as hard as they worked, food and drink being the center of their festivities. Tables were always heavily laden, not only with what they produced, but also with wild game, which was plentiful. Venison ragout was a specialty of the region.

When the war started, all that changed. Everything the country produced went to support the war effort, and food was severely rationed. The three of us in the *altenteil*, Grandmother, Mariechen, and I, received one *metwurst* sausage for the whole year. I was lucky. Grandmother would often say, "Oh, I'm just not hungry. Here, Maria, you eat this slice of *metwurst*," just like my own grandmother had done, and I would hide behind the door of the *altenteil* and gobble down the sausage. Pregnancy made my ever-present hunger even worse.

On the farm we were closely watched by inspectors who came around unannounced to check on us. If you had twenty hens you had to provide so many eggs weekly. If a sow had piglets, the inspectors would count them and keep track. If you had so many cows, you had to provide so much milk. Inspectors would come and check the fat content of milk to make sure people weren't skimming off the top. I cannot tell you the number of times Karin Huber or some other neighbor came over to Tante Grete, "Oh, Grete, may I borrow two eggs? I don't know what is the matter with my hen. She's just not laying." You had to do that because if you missed a quota, you would be in serious trouble. People were shipped off and never heard from again for such infractions. The inspectors were ruthless.

And they weren't always strangers. Many of them were locals who had been conscripted by the government, just as Uncle Otto had. It was difficult, because you would think, "I know this man. He's married to my cousin. Why is he doing this to me?" But there was no way out for them or for us.

◦◦◦

In the cities the situation was even worse. How much food do you need to support a city like Berlin with four and a half million people? The infrastructure had collapsed. Especially after the intense bombing started in late 1943, roads and railways were destroyed. Distribution centers ceased to exist. Convoys bringing food into the cities were bombed. Every morning on the farm the milk was put into cans and placed in front of the house by the side of the road. When the bombing started, if the trucks that came to collect the milk were destroyed, then the milk just sat there and soured—we were not allowed to use it. Everything was totally unpredictable.

At the very least in the country we had rutabagas and potatoes to eat. I learned to hate both. One of my jobs was to help

Grandmother peel potatoes. Being pregnant, I was not much good for anything else. For hours every day we sat outside and peeled, peeled, peeled. It was one of the most boring things I had ever done, even more boring than the dusting and cleaning Oma had made me do when I was younger. And I had to pay attention to my work. If I didn't cut the peelings paper thin, Tante Grete or Mariechen was quick to correct me. Leaving too much potato with the skin was wasting valuable food.

I was due to deliver my baby in December 1943. Normally children were born at home, especially out in the small villages and towns in the countryside. In Laaslich we had a midwife, Mrs. Kappel, who had delivered just about everyone under the age of thirty-five in the village. But she was a "mean old bitch," as Uncle Otto put it, and he was not going to subject me to her. Instead, he arranged for me to go to Dr. Koch's clinic in Wittenburge, a short distance away.

Somehow, Uncle Otto procured a car and driver to take me to the clinic when my time came. It was an old black car, probably something the local authorities used for emergency transportation. I went by myself, because no one could be spared from work on the farm. I remember Uncle Otto and Tante Grete standing there under a linden tree waving to me. As we drove away Uncle Otto shouted, "Bring us a boy!"

When I arrived, two old nurses took me in tow, and I waddled up to a room. My labor proved to be long and difficult. If it had not been for those two kindly old women, I don't think I would have made it. When Roland was finally born into a chipped enamel pan, I was totally spent. But Uncle Otto had his boy.

I returned to Laaslich after two weeks but was so weak and sick that I couldn't take care of the baby, and Uncle Otto soon took me back to the clinic with a kidney infection. I remained there a month in critical condition. I do not know how he managed, but Uncle Otto was able to contact my parents. By that time you did not travel anywhere on your own, but my father somehow managed to obtain permission to visit me.

I was in a semi-comatose state, but when I opened my eyes, there stood Tata with tears running down his cheeks. Looking through blurred eyes at my father, I thought I had died, and I'm sure he was probably thinking he was standing a deathwatch. When I finally spoke, he was beside himself with joy. Through his sobs he gave me the news, only the good, from Berlin and told me how anxious Mamá and Oma were for me and how much they loved me. The nurse allowed him only a few minutes with me, but even that few minutes with him buoyed my spirits. Over the next few weeks under Dr. Koch's care I improved rapidly and finally was able to leave the hospital.

❧❦

When I returned to the farm, I was still too weak to do anything but lie in bed. Mariechen took care of Roland, and Mrs. Kappel checked on me every day. Once I complained to her, "When am I ever going to get well? It's now been seven weeks, and I'm still so sick." She answered, "Talk to me when you're sick seven months! Seven weeks is nothing." Meanwhile, the dawn-to-dusk, back-breaking labor on the farm went on. And I returned to health.

❧❦

Not all was drudgery. Although it was illegal, most of the

farmers used potato peels to make schnapps, including Uncle Otto, who commandeered one of the laundry kettles in the wash room. One of the few Polish men happened to be an expert, and he spent a good bit of his time in the laundry room instead of the fields. I'm sure some inspectors realized what was going on, but making schnapps was widespread and didn't distract from food production, so they looked the other way. People had to have some outlet.

My salvation was that I was "exotic." There were several young women, married and unmarried, in Laaslich. Soon after my arrival, I formed a theater group in the *gasthaus,* the community center across the street next to the church. There is where we performed. Something positive to take our minds off the bleakness of our existence. We had no costumes and few backdrops, but we were creative. Our first effort was a play by the playwright Wilhelm Busch. The protagonist was Pious Helen. In my pregnant state I got to be Pious Helen, who narrated without having to move around the stage. The play was pitiful but well-received. Laaslich had never seen any entertainment like it before.

Our first production was so successful, we immediately wanted to start a second, but, because of my difficulties during and after my delivery, we were unable even to begin planning our second, Schiler's *Caesar and Cleopatra*, until the fall of 1944. Unfortunately, it never got to the stage, because the "trekkers," refugees from the east, started to arrive.

✎◦◗

We had known from wounded soldiers returning from the Eastern Front that the war was not going well there. At the same time we heard on the radio more and more reports that could only be described as propaganda, Goebels screaming that we were going to win, and that the Fuhrer had secret weapons that he was about to unleash on the Allies. In the meantime, if confronted by the enemy, women, children, and the elderly—the only ones left at home—should pour boiling water on the them, use kitchen forks to attack them. Attack. Attack. To us in Laaslich, and I'm sure elsewhere, this sounded like desperation. And in September of 1944, Hitler called up all remaining males between the ages of sixteen and sixty for army service.

There were no official reports that the Russians were advancing, but as autumn wore on and passed into winter, the trickle of refugees became a flood. These trekkers were Germans, Junkers, who had settled in East Prussia long before Hitler came to power. Many were wealthy landowners who had large estates. They had fled the Russians, leaving in ox-drawn carts—the government had long before confiscated all motor vehicles and horses—taking nothing but perhaps a few family valuables. And as they progressed and the oxen tired, they started throwing things out along the roads, which became littered with all manner of valuable things. If someone died, they had no time to bury them; they just left the bodies alongside the roads. If an old grandmother or grandfather was dying, with no hope of making it, the families put them out by the wayside to lighten the load, made them as comfortable as possible, and continued on. At first we heard only rumors of these things. Then we started getting trekkers in Laaslich.

It was incredible. There were people whose fingers were totally black from frostbite. Some would break off. Our theater group suspended its activities. Our little theater in the *gasthaus* became a refugee center, and, since I had been in charge of the theater group, I became the leader in charge of these refugees. I also became the chief cook. We used huge laundry kettles to make endless soups and stews. Everyone in the village would come by and throw in whatever they could, mostly rutabagas, but sometimes beets or potatoes, whatever they could. Occasionally, even a rabbit or an illicit chicken would end up in the kettles. The villagers were incredible in the way they shared. These people who had almost nothing and were practically starving themselves willingly shared with the trekkers, who were in desperate need.

I also took charge of the many sick, amputating fingers and toes and trying to nurse those with pneumonia and influenza back to health. It was a hopeless task. Many of them died. We buried them right there in Laaslich. The rest who lived moved on west.

We heard from the trekkers that the awful rumors about the Russians were true, how they burned everything and raped and killed, especially young women. We did not know until much later, but Stalin had issued an *ukaze*, which was a proclamation that if the "glorious Red Army" reached Berlin before the Allies, then the "glorious Red Army" could do anything it wanted. Soldiers could take anything they wanted, could rape, murder, plunder, anything.

One evening in late April with the Russians racing across east Germany the family gathered in the living room and began talking about me as if I weren't there. At first I thought we were talking about someone else. Uncle Otto was saying that the time had come when I should leave. Mariechen was against my going off alone with a seventeen-month-old baby, but Otto pointed out that the "Amis," the Americans, were close, only thirty or forty kilometers away. Once I got to the American lines I would be safe. It would take only two or three days to reach the Americans, and then, when things settled down, I could return. I was not excited about going away. I did not want to leave the family and all that was familiar to me, and I was frightened because I had never been completely on my own before, especially with a small child. But the specter of the awful Russians grew daily, and the "Amis" were just a short distance away, so I would be moving from danger to safety. Besides, the family had decided, and I had little choice.

Mariechen found an old rucksack in the barn. It probably dated from Word War I and smelled accordingly. She cut two large holes in the bottom of it for Roland's little legs, and, voilá, I had a carrier for my son. Oh, did he love it. So much fun to kick his legs, wave his arms, and sing!

On the next morning with one loaf of bread, a bit of cheese, and a tiny bit of *metwurst* that Grandmother sneaked into my coat pocket, I kissed everyone goodbye. Hoisting Roland on my back, I took one last look at the farm, stepped out with the dozens and dozens of trekkers, and started walking down the road to hell.

7

On the Road

At first, I was apprehensive. I was venturing out into the unknown and leaving behind my security. But there were so many people on the roads, hundreds, and such an air of urgency, I soon became less anxious. It wasn't that far to where the Americans were, and nothing terrible seemed to be happening. Even after all that I had been through, I was still optimistic. Soon I was exhilarated about leaving the boredom and drudgery of the farm.

It was Spring. The day was warm, the sun shining. I sang quietly to Roland and soon settled into a comfortable rhythm. Then I started looking around at others walking with me. Most appeared hungry and frightened, even terrified. None of them seemed very strong, and many were noticeably limping, just trying to put one foot in front of the other. I saw many German soldiers, arms in slings, heads swathed in bandages, some hobbling along on crutches, even some amputees. I found out that as the Eastern Front had collapsed and the Russians drove nearer, hospitals to the east had opened their doors and ordered the wounded to flee as best they could. My enthusiasm waned.

As the day wore on Roland got heavier. Because of my poor diet the last few years and the trauma I had already experienced, I was not as strong as I thought, and my endurance lagged. I started wondering why I had been so happy earlier, and I started thinking that perhaps I should have stayed on the farm and taken my chances with the Russians.

The road was crowded and progress was slow. Those thousands of shuffling feet churned up thick clouds of choking dust, and Roland now wailed constantly. My back was wet with his urine, because I had no more diapers to change him into. Possessions and refuse of all kinds littered the roads. People collapsed and fell by the wayside. By afternoon, my euphoria had disappeared, and I, too, was a frightened, fleeing refugee. As the sun set, I found some bushes a few meters off the road and collapsed behind them, exhausted. I had seen no "Amis."

I slept fitfully that night. I was so afraid of the Russians coming. And even if I had not been, Roland whimpered most of the night. All too soon, the sun rose in the east as if it were lighting the way for the Russians. Stiff and sore I got up, hoisted Roland on my back again and started walking. The sun was soon well up in the sky, and the air warmed, just like the day before. Only this day did not seem so delightful. The air heated quickly and by mid-morning it was hot. Again the road was an unbearable cloud of dust.

Once more Roland began his incessant wailing, and once more my back was soaked with his urine. By noon I was bone-weary and exhausted. It seemed as if Roland weighed a ton, but I just kept thinking of the time my tiny Oma had carried me up five flights of stairs after my bout with diphtheria in Berlin—and when I was a little girl and she had hoisted me on her back and lugged me for miles. We had been somewhere in a car, and it broke down in an isolated area. The chauffeur went off to find help, and Oma entertained me. We waited a long time, but when darkness drew near, she decided we should seek shelter for the night. I was four or five and soon tired, so she picked me up and carried me. We went for miles, and I know she must have been exhausted, but she walked on and on with me on her back until we found shelter. Now, I thought of those incidents and walked on, too, carrying Roland as Oma had carried me.

In the early afternoon there was shouting from behind, and the flow of this human river I was in seemed to increase. In fact, a flash flood of humanity pushed us forward from the rear. And then came the cries, "The Russians are coming! The Russians are coming!" Sure enough, I heard the deep-throated rumble and clanking of tanks above the commotion on the road.

I ran off to find a place to hide and finally fell behind a clump of bushes a short distance away. I was trembling with fear as I watched a wounded German soldier stagger down the road calling for help. He was holding his stomach, sutures broken. I could see his intestines hanging out. As he wobbled painfully along a Russian tank came roaring down the road and overtook him. It never slowed down. The treads of the tank ground him into the heavy dust of the road. Then another tank ran over him. And another. And another. By the time they all had passed, the soldier was hardly a greasy lump in the road. I lay there behind those bushes sobbing and shaking and vomiting. No one else got back out on the road for a long time.

Finally, word filtered forward that Russian infantry were now not far behind us, so the people around me and I ran off farther into the woods and headed northwest again, paralleling the road. I ran as fast as I could. Roland was heavy and bouncing up and down and screaming, but I ran. I ran and ran until I finally dropped, completely spent and gasping.

After a time I willed myself back on my feet along with the others in our little group and started walking again, always looking over my shoulder for the Russians, always fearing they would overtake us. Someone said that the "Amis" were in Eldena, not so far away, and Eldena became our mecca. I really had no idea where we were going; I just followed the person ahead of me. My child screamed. My knees and feet ached. My legs felt like lead weights. My mind drifted. But I kept putting one foot in front of the other. Many times in the coming months I found myself in similar circumstances, trudging down endless roads, but that trek to Eldena sticks in my mind like it was yesterday.

Finally, I collapsed in some underbrush next to a tree at the edge of a forest just as night was descending. Even Roland had exhausted himself and had fallen asleep. I carefully took him from my back, laid down with him cradled in my arms, and covered us both up with my coat. I was asleep in seconds.

Just at dawn I awoke with a start to Roland's screaming and gunfire—all around us and even above us. We were right in the middle of a battle between an SS unit, many of whom were up in the trees, and the Russian infantry, which was firing and advancing into the tree line. SS soldiers were dropping everywhere. Some of the civilians I was with got up and tried to run but were immediately cut down by Russian rifle fire. Shooting, screaming, smoke, bloody bodies everywhere. An SS soldier fell out of a tree right on top of us, which only made Roland wail all the louder. I smelled and felt the blood of the dead soldier soaking my back.

Eventually the firing died down, and I could hear the Russians moving toward me, could hear them talking excitedly to each other. I stuffed a glove in Roland's mouth to silence his crying. That was all I could think to do. I could hear the Russians bayoneting all the bodies. I could hear the live ones scream as they were being stabbed. I had to play dead. A Russian soldier, I could smell him, stopped next to me and the dead German lying on top of me. He kicked the German and then kicked me. When he was satisfied we were both dead, he moved on. I barely breathed. Poor little Roland. He was quivering.

I stayed there not moving and hardly breathing for most of the morning, even though it was deathly quiet in the woods. About midday I forced the body off me and cautiously looked around before I got up. Thank God, Roland was still breathing. I sat up and held him close to me, rocking him back and forth for a long time. By then, he wasn't shaking. He just lay in my arms and didn't even whimper.

Finally, I found the strength to stand. Roland and I were the only living beings there. The stench of death was pervasive. Many German soldiers lay all around in grotesque positions. All of the civilians I had been with had been shot or bayoneted, or they had managed to slip away. I felt as if Roland and I were the last two people alive on earth. But I couldn't stay there forever. I gathered up my courage and went around to the bodies of the German soldiers and the few Russians to search for food and water. Roland and I ate quickly, and, taking what items I could carry, I put him on my back and headed toward what I thought would be Eldena.

I trudged on during the rest of that day and eventually met up with other civilian refugees like myself. I was exhausted and filthy and covered with blood, but I was no longer alone. Even though I didn't know them, they were a great comfort to me. As night fell we again just dropped where we were. I still had food and water left which I had taken from the dead soldiers, and I shared that with the others. We worried about being caught by the Russians again, but we hadn't seen any all day long, and that was at least a little reassuring. We all fell instantly into an exhausted sleep.

In the morning we again arose and with our last energy struggled forward toward our goal, Eldena. In the late afternoon we came out of the woods near an intersection of two roads. And beyond the intersection we could see a village. It was Eldena. We were safe.

The first place our small band came to was a farm at the edge of town. We wandered wearily into the yard, where a woman met us. "You can sleep in the barn," she said. "I don't have any food, but there's water and hay to sleep in." I was so grateful just to be there and have a roof over my head and a safe place to sleep, I didn't care about not having any food. I could have kissed her.

We all headed toward the barn, but when the lady saw me with Roland, she motioned me aside. "You come stay in the house," she said to me, I suppose because I had a child. Then this very kind woman brought us some milk and bread. Roland and I drank greedily from the big bowl of milk she gave us and I broke off small chunks of bread, dipped them with my dirty hands into the milk, and stuffed them into little Roland's mouth. He ate hungrily.

After we had eaten our fill, she said, "I'm sorry I cannot offer you a bed, because there aren't any left, but at least you don't have to sleep in the barn." I'll never forget that. She gave us some blankets, and we went into the entryway. It had a gray flagstone floor. Lying on those hard stones was wonderful. We were under a roof. No one was shooting and screaming and dying around us. There was no danger of a dead soldier's body falling on us, no danger of someone stabbing us with a bayonet. And no need to stuff anything into Roland's mouth. Never mind that I was filthy. The only thing that mattered was that my child and I were alive and safe. Our stomachs were full. We had shelter. That is what I was thinking as I fell into a deep sleep.

8

Barbarians

I awoke slowly the next morning. I could feel Roland cuddled against me, and I could sense sunlight through my closed eyelids. But there was something else—a smell. And I heard men talking and laughing. They weren't speaking English or German. Slowly I opened my eyes to the boots and brown pant legs of a Russian uniform straddling me. I looked up into the grinning face of a drunken Russian soldier leering down at me. And I could see others standing in the doorway behind him.

During the night the Americans had pulled back across the Elde River, which runs through the center of Eldena, and the Russian Army had moved in. These troops were Mongolians with Russian officers, and they were beasts, no different from the hordes of Genghis Khan, no different from their barbarian ancestors in the Middle Ages. They came from a culture so foreign to the rest of the world. They had no sense of personal hygiene, no morals, no compassion, no human decency whatever. And on top of that, Stalin had given them leave to do anything they wanted.

CROSSING THE ELDE BRIDGE

I rose up on my elbows and tried to slide backwards, pulling Roland with me, but the soldier kicked me viciously in the side, and I screamed in pain. He and the others roared with laughter. Then he began unbuttoning his fly and pulling down his pants. I kicked up between his legs as hard as I could with little effect, and he dropped to his knees and smashed me in the face with his fist. I guess I was momentarily knocked out, because when I came to, he had pulled off the blanket, raised my dress, and ripped off my filthy panties, and he was inside me, slamming brutally against my groin. He finished quickly and stood up, slapping me hard for good measure. Then the next one took me and the next. They were standing in line. They twisted my arms and legs, hit me and kicked me, all the time laughing. It was great fun for these monsters. I was so traumatized and the pain was so overpowering that I could not move. I was in shock. When they had all finished—I don't remember how many there were—they all stood around laughing and urinating on my face.

The physical pain was absolutely horrendous. But the emotional trauma was…I cannot describe my feelings. I wished I could have died. Right then I wished I could have died. If I ever saw my husband again, how could I ever make love to him? And if I ever saw my parents again, how could I look into their faces? I felt so dirty and somehow so guilty. I could not speak of this for fifty years to anyone, not to anyone. For fifty years I carried this pain inside me. I was the lowest of creatures.

When the soldiers were through with me a few left, but some of them sat or squatted down in corners and fell asleep or defecated right in the house. These Mongolians. The stench. The foulest odors from their mouths, their bodies. They were constantly drinking—to the point of vomiting—and they never brushed their teeth, never washed, never changed clothes.

I just lay there, motionless. How could I ever stand up after this? How could I ever walk again? After a time, the remaining soldiers drifted out by ones and twos, and I was left alone. Then Roland started crying. He was hungry, and he had dirtied his diapers. I had nothing to change him into, but I cleaned him as best I could and fed him the little bit of bread we had left.

At that moment the lady who owned the house staggered into the entry way. She too had been raped and beaten, and her house was a shambles. She was terribly distraught and said, "You have to go. You have to go." Because having any other young women there in the house would attract more soldiers, more trouble for her. I was the magnet, and so I had to leave. She did tell me that there were empty houses down the road. Many people had fled when the Russians entered the town and I would find refuge in one of the vacated homes, but I could not stay there. So I struggled to my feet, picked up Roland, and left.

I found a house four doors down that had not been ransacked and went inside. I was so worried, not only about the extreme physical discomfort I was suffering and the good possibility that I would be raped again, but also about venereal disease. I was educated enough to know that some sort of disease was a real possibility, and I could do nothing to prevent it. Inside the house I called out. No one answered. I walked around the rooms. Nothing had been touched. In the cellar I had the good fortune to find some canned food, meats and fruit. And in the kitchen I found a small piece of lye soap. I washed Roland and myself as best I could with the lye soap in the sink, and then I put the soap inside me. I almost passed out from the searing pain, because I had literally been torn apart. I had to choke down a scream, but I did it, and I did the same every time I had a chance later.

I fed Roland, ate a little myself, and then went upstairs to a room where there were beds. I was completely exhausted. I put Roland on a bed and lay down beside him. We both were fast asleep almost immediately. We stayed in that house a day or two, but again, the Russians found me. I was once more beaten and raped unmercifully. And once again, I took my little sliver of lye soap, cleaned myself, and then fled with Roland to find another hiding place.

Carrying Roland in my arms I went out the back door and down the lane, praying that I would not run into any Russian soldiers. Not far down the lane I saw a house that looked empty and not too damaged. I also heard Mongolian voices coming from behind the house on the other side of the lane. I quickly ducked into the front door of the house and quietly closed and locked it. I stood there for a few moments trying to catch my breath when a man appeared from the back of the house. I gave a little whimper, thinking that I had once again been caught and would be abused, but he motioned to me, "It's okay. It's okay." Then he said almost in a whisper, "I'm German. I'm trying to hide, too." He was a young man, perhaps nineteen or twenty. I think he had been a soldier and had been wounded and so was either sent home or had left one of the hospitals when they emptied out all the patients as the Russians were advancing.

I wanted to go look for a bed, but he said, "No, no," and he took me out to the barn behind the house. The barn had a hayloft filled with hay, and he took Roland and me there, pulled out some hay, and directed me into the space, shifting the hay back in place. Others had obviously hidden there before. Then he left.

Not long after, I heard a commotion below. The Russians were outside and soon entered the barn. The young man was with them. I could hear them screaming at him, "*Frau! Frau!*" meaning where is the woman? He did not betray me. It was terribly stuffy covered with so much hay as we were, absolutely no air, and, of course, Roland tried to cry. I once again stuffed a rag into his mouth. I could hear someone coming up the ladder. Then I could smell him and hear him sticking his bayonet into the hay, trying to find anyone hiding there. I was sitting there with Roland, holding a rag in his mouth, trying to calm him, my heart pounding so loudly I thought the Russian would hear it. But there was a lot of other noise. The soldiers below were cursing and breaking things, and the young man was saying in German that there was no one there while the Russians kept screaming, "*Frau! Frau!*" I suppose someone must have seen me go into the house earlier or perhaps saw me running down the lane in this general direction. Finally, it was quiet, although I didn't know if all the Russians had left, so I sat there all night keeping Roland still.

Early the next morning, someone came into the barn and started up the ladder to the hayloft. I was petrified. I heard the hay being moved and thought, oh my God, this is it, but it was only the young German. He was carrying an old pot filled with fresh milk. Both Roland and I drank it all down. All the while he was whispering to me to be very quiet. After we had finished the milk, the young man left, and we fell back asleep.

When it was dark again, the young German returned. "Be quiet," he whispered. "They're right outside. You have to get out of here. They suspect something, so you must leave." We climbed down the ladder, careful not to make any sound, and he showed me the way out the back. As stealthily as I could, I clutched Roland close to my chest and hurried into the woods behind the barn and stayed there until the next day.

9

On the Run

And so I spent my days moving from hiding place to hiding place, living like a rat, trying to avoid the Russians and always on the lookout for food. Since so many people had fled the town as the Russians moved in, many houses had at least a little food that the occupants had left as they fled, most often canned vegetables and fruits stored in the cellars. There was not a lot, because the previous years of war had taken its toll, but there were at least a few jars in most of the homes. The only problem was that as the Russians moved around and entered more and more homes, they usually ate whatever they found themselves or broke the jars.

We hid in cramped spaces, listened in fear for the approach of any Russians, searched through dank, dark cellars for food, watched from attic windows. And some of the sights I saw turn my stomach to this day.

Roland and I were hiding in the attic of a house near the river on the outskirts of town. Getting in and out was difficult, but we didn't have to be quite so quiet. A small window on one end of the attic was open, letting in fresh air. Roland was sleeping, and I was sitting there, looking out the window, enjoying the morning sunshine, when several Russian soldiers came into view herding a small group of old people and a pregnant woman. The soldiers were laughing, playfully jabbing these people with their bayonets. The Russians were obviously drunk. They stopped at the next house about fifty yards away and set fire to the thatched roof. Then they forced the Germans to carry buckets down to the river. It was pitiful to watch that pregnant woman and those old people staggering under the weight of those buckets of water. While the Germans fetched the water, two of the Russians put a ladder up against the house. The first German back to the house was an old man. The soldiers forced him up the ladder, but he was so weak he fell off about halfway up. The soldiers shot him and laughed. Then the young pregnant woman arrived, and they forced her up the ladder. She was stronger and she reached the top with her bucket of water, which she threw on the fire. Before she could climb back down, the soldiers began shaking the ladder until she fell—into the fire. She screamed for a time and then was quiet. The soldiers laughed hysterically.

❦

And the cattle. Almost everyone in that area raised cows, Holsteins. Eldena was a farming community, and there were cows everywhere. Another entertainment the Russians had was to shoot these cows, but they would not kill them outright. They would use them for target practice and just wound them. Then the poor beasts would bellow in agony. The Russians seemed to love sitting there listening to the wretched creatures die.

No one was allowed to take the meat. The Russians took

some, of course, but there was so much. All the German citizens could do was watch as the carcasses rotted away, covered with flies and maggots, stinking so badly it made everyone nauseous.

There also was the Elde River, Russians on one side, Americans on the other. Dead bodies, animal and human, continually float-ed downstream. The smell was unbearable. And what was even worse, young women on the Russian side who could not take it anymore would place their babies in the grass along the river bank and jump in to drown themselves. I couldn't stand to see that, because I came so close to doing the same thing myself.

One day the Russians passed the word around town that the bridge across the river to the American side would be open at three o'clock in the afternoon for twenty minutes for anyone who wished to cross over. My heart leaped with joy. I was going to get away from these beasts. When the sun was directly overhead, I took Roland to the bridge and we waited in the shade of a huge chestnut tree nearby. As the afternoon wore along, more and more people came. One man had a watch, and at three o'clock we all crowded around with great anticipation. The guards at the bridge angrily pushed us back. Ten minutes passed, then twenty. Nothing. Finally, two motorcycles drove up and the motorcyclists muscled their way through the crowd and onto the bridge. They stopped and turned around. Then they dismounted, pulled out submachine guns, and started firing into the crowd, laughing up-roariously. Amid the screams and deafening noise I fell to the ground with Roland and managed somehow to crawl behind the chestnut tree and away. I don't know how many were killed, but dozens of bodies just laid there for several days until the stench got so bad the Russians pushed them into the river.

～∂∞～

Following that incident I found a very nicely furnished house that was empty and not vandalized. The owners obviously were well-to-do. Strangely, there was a bed in the living room. Perhaps one of the occupants had been an invalid. I made sure no one was there, then I went into the cellar and found a large quantity of canned foods, again mostly fruits and vegetables, but there were also some canned meats. I took as many jars as I could carry and went upstairs.

Before he told me to leave, the kind young man in the barn had told me to push heavy furniture against the doors of the houses I would be hiding in. The Russians probably would not come in if they had to work at opening the door. There were so many other places for them to ransack. So that is what I did. With much effort I pushed a heavy dresser up against the door. Then Roland and I ate until we were both stuffed. The rest of the day and that night passed without incident, and that bed felt so wonderful.

The next day there was shouting at the door, "*Davai! Davai!*" I did not breathe. I did not move. There was no place to escape, nowhere to hide. I prayed that the dresser would be too hard to move and the soldiers would give up, but they didn't, and I finally heard the dresser scraping along the floor. Then they streamed in. I do not know how many there actually were.

The soldiers ran all through the house smashing things and discovered the jars of food, which they opened and urinated in or broke outright until they ran out of jars. When they had destroyed everything, they laughed uproariously and squatted down in the corners of the living room, which seemed filled with jars of urine and broken glass.

Then the raping started. The bed was against the wall, and Roland was lying on the inside; I didn't want him to fall out. He had been sleeping, but when the soldiers came into the house he woke up and started squirming and wailing. One of them grabbed Roland and threw him viciously on the floor. I screamed and tried to reach for him, but the soldier smashed me in the face.

Again, if I had had some way to kill myself, I would have. I think I stepped outside the reality of the moment. I could not defend myself, and these animals were taking me, one after the other. Finally, there was a little peace. I lay on the bed semi-conscious, bleeding, my child dead on the floor, or so I thought.

Suddenly, in walked another soldier. And I thought, oh, my God, not another one. I cannot. I cannot. Dear God, let me die. But he was an officer, decorations on his chest. When he came in he saw all the soldiers lying around and started yelling at them and kicking them, as they scrambled out the broken-down door. Then he came over to the bed where I lay, and I thought, "How can I make my heart stop beating. How can I stop breathing?" But he bent down to pick Roland up, laying him close beside me. And, thank God, Roland was still alive.

Then the officer sat directly on the bed and said, "Don't be afraid. Don't be afraid, Little Dove, I'm not going to hurt you. I am so sorry for what they did to you. You are so young. I'm so sorry."

And I couldn't believe this. I still thought that this was some kind of ruse, and as soon as I responded, he would laugh in my face. But he didn't. He said, "Really, I am not going to hurt you. I would like to help you. This is going to be terrible here. It isn't going to stop. I have to leave at one thirty this afternoon, and I'd like to take you and the child with me. At one o'clock I will be in the Komandantura. You can come and look for me, and I'll take you with me."

And like the very proper young lady that I was and in spite of everything that had already happened to me, I told him that I was sorry, but I could not go with him. "I'm a married woman."

"Well, think about it," and he gave me his name. "If you change your mind, I'll be very happy to take you with me, and, if you are with me, I will protect you."

10

Death Sentence

I lay there paralyzed. This seemed to be my only chance to escape, but after what had just happened to me, how could I trust a Russian? The officer repaired the door and told me to stack more furniture up against it. With a final, "Well, if you change your mind, come to the Komandantura by one o'clock," he turned and left.

I was so exhausted and weak I could barely move, but I managed to get the dresser back in place against the door and then lay down next to Roland, who was still whimpering.

Not long after the Russian officer left, more soldiers pounded on the door. I lay on the bed, unable to think, unable to move. Soon, I heard the scraping of the heavy furniture along the floor as they forced the door open, and I was staring at two more drunken Mongolians. When they finished with me, they left, leaving the door wide open. My insides felt as if they were ripped apart, and I was on fire. But worst of all, my mind and my soul was smashed into a thousand pieces.

CROSSING THE ELDE BRIDGE

After these last two, I thought this has to stop. I cannot go on like this. Anything would be better than this. If I have to live with that Russian officer as his woman, it cannot be as bad as being raped and beaten by these horrible animals and being shot at and constantly running and hiding. I am going to find him. I do not care where he is going.

I had no idea what time it was, because I had long since lost my watch, as well as my wedding ring and the gold necklace Jurgen had given to me. I staggered down the street with Roland in my arms. When I got to the Komandantura, I found to my dismay that the Russian officer had left. What was I to do now? Locate another empty house and start over.

I retraced my steps, although I could hardly walk, but I had to find some shelter and hopefully something to eat. Unfortunately, down the street came two more Russian soldiers, leering at me. As they approached, I feverishly tried to think what to do. Then it came to me. I spoke Croatian, a Slavic language somewhat like Russian. Maybe I could make them understand, and they would have pity on me.

In Croatian I said, "Please, please, no. I am your sister." They stopped short and looked at me, then yelled angrily, "*Ti špion! Ti špion!*" "You're a spy! You're a spy!" To them only people who worked for the KGB and spies spoke more than one language, so I was a spy, and they took me back to the Komandantura. Still holding Roland, I was taken into a room where a Russian officer sat behind a desk. He questioned me briefly and kept asking for whom I was spying. Of course, I could not answer that, since I was not a spy. He became very angry and soon ordered me to be sent to the prison, a two-story house beside the river near the Komandantura. A guard took Roland and me there and threw us into a crowded room on the first floor.

During the next few days, I was interrogated several times, usually at night. Guards would come and pull me out of the room, leaving Roland behind. I never knew if I would ever return. I had nothing to confess, so they beat me, kicked me, kept me from sleeping. Within days I felt like a zombie from lack of sleep. I was starving. Some of my ribs were broken. My body was crawling with lice. And there were continual screams and moans from various parts of the building because, I supposed, many people were being beaten and tortured as I was.

One day a soldier came into the room where we prisoners had been placed, looked around, and motioned to me. I carefully picked up Roland and went to the door. The soldier handed me a shovel and said, "Come with me." Adrenalin rushed through my veins. My heart slammed against my chest so hard that my broken ribs and sore muscles throbbed in pain. This was it. I was going to die. What would happen to Roland? Would they kill him too?

I followed the soldier out the back door of the house and into the large yard behind. The air was cool, but it was a beautiful day. The azure sky reminded me of Dalmatia. My heart ached. A soft breeze made the pink and yellow flowers dance and carried their fragrance across the lot. At the back, we stopped and he motioned for me to put Roland down by a nearby bush. Then he pointed to a spot and told me to start digging. My knees went weak, and I gasped. Was I digging my own grave? I turned toward him and pleaded, "Please, please. My baby." He yelled angrily at me and jabbed with his bayonet. "Dig! Dig!" The stench of dead cattle replaced the fragrance of the flowers. I pulled myself together and started digging.

It took me a long time. My arms and legs, my whole body,

burned with the effort. Finally, I had a shallow grave dug, fully expecting that in the next few minutes I would be lying dead in it. But as I stood there breathing hard and perspiring from my labor, another Russian guard approached roughly pushing a blindfolded German soldier with his hands tied behind his back. His coat had been removed—the Russians were so poorly clothed, they salvaged everything they could—and he wore only a tattered shirt and trousers. He was barefoot. I couldn't tell how old he was because of the blindfold, and his unshaven face was drawn and dirty. I could smell his fear as the guard positioned him at one end of the grave and jabbed him behind his knees to make him kneel.

Rivulets of sweat ran down his face, and his lips moved frantically making wheezing sounds. I could not hear what he was saying, so I don't know if he was praying or cursing his fate. He just knelt there mumbling unintelligibly and trembling. I could feel his agony. Then the Russian guard stuck the muzzle of his rifle close to the German's neck and fired.

The back of the German soldier's neck exploded in a fountain of blood, and he pitched forward into the grave. He lay there a few seconds twitching, and in one final gasp moaned, "*Mutti!*" "Momma." Then he was still. Vomit welled up into my throat, and I turned away, but one of the Russian soldiers grabbed my shoulder, pointed at the shovel then at the bloody corpse. My job wasn't finished. As I shoveled dirt into the hole, I said a silent prayer for this young man and asked his forgiveness. When I finished, the Russians motioned me back to the house. I picked up Roland, who lay whimpering under the bush, and walked back across the yard. As we entered, birds started singing again, and I took one last look at the blue sky.

DEATH SENTENCE

The next day, I was called in for interrogation and the officer who began talking to me seemed like a nice man. He asked, "Have you been fed well?" and I thought a moment before I admitted, "No, I have not been fed today."

"What?" he yelled. "This girl has not been fed. That is outrageous," he ranted. "Bring her some food immediately."

I thought, oh God, this man will be my savior. A soldier came in with a little tin plate with a fish on it, a salted fish. I was so stupid and so hungry, I took the fish and devoured the whole thing. Then, of course, I was terribly thirsty and I asked for some water.

The officer smiled. "As soon as you confess. Not a drop before."

"Please," I begged.

"When you confess."

"I do not have anything to confess."

"You are a spy. What were you assignments?"

"I am not a spy! I have not had any assignments!"

"You are going to tell me right now or else!"

Believe me, if I could have made up something, I would have. If I had known enough about espionage work, I would have lied just to get out of that situation, but I did not.

"Okay, that's it. You are going to die. Take her away."

And I was dragged away to an upstairs room where those sentenced to death were held.

11

Escape

On the way upstairs someone handed Roland to me. As soon as I got to the room, the guard made me strip, because, if you were condemned to death, the Russians did not want to waste any clothing that might be of use. So I took off my clothes, which were thrown on a pile in a corner.

I do not remember how many people were in that upstairs room, maybe twelve or fifteen, all stark naked. I do remember that there was an old woman with six or seven little ones. I do not think they could have been her own children; they may have been her grandchildren. I couldn't imagine why they were there. I did not ask. No one talked, partly because we were all naked and partly because no one had anything left to say. We were all going to die. Words were useless at such a time. We had lost all hope.

I was lying on a cot with Roland and was in a state between sleep and wakefulness. I was also thinking of the execution of the German soldier I had witnessed. Would they kill Roland with me? I had heard that if you had a child you were expected to kneel and to hold it against your breast, and then the soldiers would shoot you in the back. You could only pray that the bullet would kill you and your child. In any case, I knew that the next morning I would be dead. I would never see my husband again. I would never see my parents or grandmother again. I would never see the blue sky. I would never smell a flower. And what would happen to Roland if he was taken from me? All that was going through my mind. I was resigned to my death, and I wanted to die as quickly as possible. No more pain. No more humiliation. Only peace, forever.

Then I heard voices which seemed far off, and my first thought was, "Oh, they're here. It's daylight already. It's time." I prayed that Roland and I would both die from the one bullet. Then I realized that one voice I heard was not Russian, just like that first morning in Eldena when I had heard a strange voice that I knew was not English. This was in reverse. The voice was speaking a strange English, unlike the Oxford English I had been taught. I opened my eyes, and there stood an American soldier with his back toward me.

A Russian, who was guarding this room of the condemned, stood next to him, and the American was giving the Russian cigarettes, chocolate, and chewing gum. The Russian held his hand out for more. The American was standing slightly turned between me and the Russian with his back to me, and I could see his pistol hanging on his right hip. The holster flap was not fastened. He was so close. I realized that I could end our misery, if I could just get that pistol. I reached out quietly and started to remove it. At that moment something hit my arm and the gun fired. The shot went into the wall, just missing the American's back.

He had whirled around and gripped my wrist very tightly,

twisting the gun from my hand. The Russian just stood there and laughed. I was in such a complete state of desperation and agony, that I began speaking rapidly in French to the American. "Please, please, sir. Kill me and my son now. Please. Please. Shoot us right now," I pleaded.

And just as rapidly he replied in French, "No. I promise you. I'll get you out of here."

I was shocked. How many American GIs spoke such fluent French? But what was he saying? He didn't know me, and it would be impossible to get me away from the Russians. No, I had lost my last chance to kill myself. That would have been my liberation, to end it. And now that was taken away from me.

The American turned back to the Russian, and they continued their haggling. When it seemed that the Russian had taken just about everything the American had to offer, he dropped his hand and grinned. Then, pointing to his watch, he indicated twenty minutes. The American had me for twenty minutes. Then the Russian left and closed the door.

The room was filled with people, but in spite of that, the sad truth which hurts me to this day is that the American also raped me. Here was an American, the man who said he would get me out of there—and he raped me.

When he finished, he immediately went to the corner where the clothing was piled, rifled through the stack, and finally pulled out a coat which he handed to me. "Put it on," he said in English. "We have only a few minutes."

"What are you going to do?"

"I'm going to get you out of here. I told you that." He looked out the window. "There's a trellis and a downspout on this side of the house. I'll take the boy and climb down first. Now, do exactly as I say."

I did not want to give Roland to him, but at that point I had no choice. Before I knew it the American had Roland in his arms and was out the window and climbing down. I put the coat on over my naked body and quickly followed. Within seconds we were on the ground, and he was pulling me by the hand through the shadows toward the bridge.

When we got near, we stopped to survey our surroundings. He whispered again in English, "Look. That guard on the bridge is not going to want to let you through. I still have some cigarettes, chewing gum, and chocolate. And I also have a pearl-handled pistol. These guys love weapons, and as a last resort I'll offer him the gun. Watch carefully. If he says 'yes' anytime during our little conversation, you run. Run as fast as you can across that bridge and don't stop until you get to our sentry over there. I'll be right behind you. If he still says 'no' after I offer him the gun, you fly even faster, because I'm going to shoot the bastard. Understand?"

"Yes," I said. "I understand."

"Oh, and just so you know, my name is Tom Bates."

He handed Roland to me and we stood there for some time watching. The moon was almost full, and there was the great chestnut tree, blossoms bright white in the moonlight, right next to the river. The guard wandered back and forth, smoking and mostly staring into the water. He looked bored. Another guard was leaning against the side of the bridge snoring.

After a long while, we came out of the shadows and approached the Mongolian guard, who grinned at us. Tom started conversing in broken German.

"Comrade, Stalin good."

ESCAPE

The Russian grinned again. "Roosevelt good." President Roosevelt was dead by that time, but the Russian did not know it. He pointed at me. "*Frau.*"

"Yes. *Frau. Amerikanska.*" Tom pulled me toward him.

The Russian continued grinning. "Comrade, Roosevelt good. Stalin good. *Frau* here." He was not going to let me leave.

This went on for quite a while. Tom kept handing him cigarettes, then chewing gum, and then all the chocolate he had. Still, the Russian would not budge. I stood behind Tom holding Roland, intent on every word, because they were deciding my life.

Finally, Tom pulled out the shiny pistol and held it in the palm of his hand. It glistened in the moonlight. The Russian gasped and his eyes widened. "Comrade. Roosevelt good. Stalin good." And he reached out to take the offered pistol. "I take." I darted around Tom and the Russian, clutching Roland tightly to my chest, and raced for the other side. I could hear Tom behind me. We flew across that bridge.

About a block and a half away from the bridge we were stopped by an American officer. I was still breathless and elated. Tom tried to explain what had happened, but the officer curtly cut him off. "I'll deal with you later." Then, to me, "Your papers, please."

My good spirits evaporated. I said, "Sir, I don't have any papers."

"Then, go right back. You're going right back across the bridge."

"I'm not going back," I replied.

We argued back and forth for several minutes. Finally, completed exasperated, he demanded, "Show me your papers or you're going back this instant."

I stood my ground and looked squarely at him. "Sir, if you order me to go across that bridge with my child, I will not. I'll go into the river."

And he knew exactly what that meant, because he too had heard the splashes in the river and seen the bodies floating downstream and heard the babies crying on the far bank. He stopped cold and stared at the river. Finally he said, "All right, but I'm putting you under arrest right away."

A moment later two soldiers drove up in a jeep and took Roland and me to a farmhouse on the western outskirts of town. Fortunately for Tom, they did not punish him. He apparently was one of the unit's communicators and their only cryptographer, so they could not afford to lose him.

⚬⚬

Tom was an interesting character. In the following weeks he told me that he was a paratrooper, and his unit, which now occupied the west bank of the Elde River, had fought through Italy, including the bitter fighting around Monte Cassino. They had been strictly forbidden to cross the bridge to the Russian side, but before the war Tom had owned a little newspaper in New England, and as a journalist he was very curious. He heard the cries and the shots that came from the other side of the river, he smelled the stench, and he saw the bodies floating down the Elde. So one night he talked a friend of his, who was standing guard at the bridge, into letting him cross over. He said he would be gone only a couple of hours. He wanted to find out what was going on.

Tom had seen the house at one end of the street along the

river and the barbed wire around the back of it, so that's where he went. The Russian guard at the entrance thought he was looking for a woman. *"Frau? Frau?"* And he indicated that there was a young woman upstairs. Tom gave him a pack of cigarettes, and the guard let him in and directed him up the stairs. I guess when he saw a naked young woman, he thought it was too good to be true.

I am grateful to him to this day but also hurt and saddened by his behavior. He turned out to be a nice man. War does strange things to people.

12

With the Americans

The officer who had stopped Tom and me rode with us to the farmhouse, which was to be my "prison," and posted a guard, a tall skinny boy from Texas. I could hardly understand his accent. He showed me to a room in an unoccupied part of the house and asked, "Ma'am, would y'all lak somethin' ta eat?"

I had to think for a bit to decipher what he said. Finally, I answered that we would.

"Wul, ah'm sorry, but all we got is powdered eggs."

"That will be fine," I said, even though I'd never heard of such a thing as powdered eggs.

And off he went to the kitchen and scrambled us some eggs. Roland and I both devoured them. Roland promptly threw up. Then the young soldier brought in a washtub, clean towels, and a bar of Lux soap. I could not believe it—real soap. I had not had a bath since I'd left Laaslich. So, I thought, well, the Americans at least want their women clean when they rape them. The incident with Tom seemed somehow separate. The young soldier reappeared with buckets of hot water, and when he had filled the tub, he said, "Okay, someone will be here at nine in the morning to pick y'all up." Then he handed me the key to the room so I could lock it, turned, and left. I just stood there staring at the key in my hand. How is this possible, I thought. When is the rape going to take place? I was so accustomed to this horror I could not believe that anyone could be such a polite and decent human being.

That night Roland and I went to sleep in a big bed with clean sheets and a fluffy comforter and pillows, and the door to the room was locked, and there was no screaming and shooting. I thought we were in Heaven. We slept like two stones.

In the morning our young Texan brought us hot food from the Officers' Mess, and the lady who owned the farm brought in two liters of milk. I asked, "What is this?"

She was not very friendly, I guess because I was with the Americans. "They told me to bring you two liters of milk every morning. Here it is."

"But, we can't drink all of that. Please just leave a little for us. I'm sure there are German children who need it."

"They told me to bring two liters. Here it is." She set the pot down and left.

Shortly before nine o'clock, a jeep drove up with four soldiers in it. They knocked on my door, and when I opened it they handed me a package. They had broken into the only clothing store on the west side of the river and had picked out a red and blue flowered dress for me. And there was underwear—it did not fit but who cared—shoes for my poor blistered feet, and even lipstick, although I did not wear it. There were also clothes for Roland.

WITH THE AMERICANS

I quickly got dressed, dressed Roland, and went out. Three of the soldiers stayed to look after Roland, and I left with the driver. I went with some trepidation because of the Russians, but I knew that Roland would be safe with these GIs. And to have a clean body and decent clothes was a luxury beyond imagining.

The driver took me to a hotel, the only hotel in Eldena. The Americans were using it for their headquarters. He escorted me inside to a room with big leather chairs. There was coffee, cigarettes, and pastry. At first I thought, something is terribly wrong here. This is not as it should be. What do they expect of me? What are they going to do with me? There were several soldiers there, all officers, I think. They were very nice and pleasant. We just sat around talking, and they asked me a lot of questions. Why did I speak so many languages so well? I explained that.

They asked me about Hitler. I had seen Hitler only once and that was at a railroad station in Berlin when I still had to work for the Nazis. I was standing on the platform, and all of a sudden dozens of guards flooded the place and made everyone stand where they were. Then a train came in very slowly, and Hitler stood there waving. He was only about twenty feet away. He had very penetrating blue eyes. When the train stopped he was escorted away between double flanks of guards. I told the Americans that was the only time I had ever seen the man.

They asked me about Hermann Goering. How was it when Goering brought the entire Deutsche Oper from Berlin to Karinhall, his big estate named after his first wife? I didn't know, I had never met the man. They asked me about my life history. I told them everything—except, of course, my eight months at Spandau. When I expressed my interest in the theater and opera, even telling them that I had wanted to sing opera, they asked me again how it was when Goering brought the Deutsche Oper to Karinhall. I told them again that I had never been there.

For three days they questioned me, asking the same questions over and over again in different ways, trying to catch me in a lie. Of course, I never lied to them. Their interrogations were always relaxed and friendly, but they were purposeful, and there was a certain amount of underlying tension. They knew what they were doing. Finally, they said that they would bring in a man who spoke Croatian, and we could have a nice conversation.

In came a tall, dark-haired soldier. He whispered something to the officers and then glared at me. "*Kuća!*"

I answered, "House!"

After a few moments, he said, "*Konj.*"

I replied, "Horse."

Then he said, "*Majka.*"

I said, "Mother."

Finally, he turned around, whispered something to the officers, and left the room. One of the officers looked at me and said, "You passed the test."

"I beg your pardon?"

"You passed the test, miss."

"But I thought I was to have a conversation with this gentleman."

The officer laughed, "Well, that was it."

I suppose after three days they knew me well enough and were satisfied that I was not a spy. That was my introduction to the Americans.

❧

The next day the officer who had "arrested" me said he

needed an interpreter and asked me to accompany him. He did not say where. Roland was to stay at the farmhouse with the soldiers—who were spoiling him rotten. With other soldiers the officer took me to the small village of Ludwigslust. Nearby in the middle of nowhere was a concentration camp, Reierhorst. I believe most of the people in Ludwigslust and the surrounding area knew nothing of this camp. People were so frightened they did not want to know anything. And, of course, there were many barbed wire fences and minefields surrounding the camp, so no one would even think of going near the place.

In Hamburg there was a very big concentration camp called Neuengamme. So little was heard of it in America, but Neuengamme was notorious. It was as big and as horrendous as Dachau. From Neuengamme the Nazis would send prisoners to Reierhorst and from Reierhorst…

We arrived at the camp early in the morning. It was surrounded by a high wooden fence and a wooden gate. The American soldiers tried and tried to open the gate, but they could not budge it. Finally, they called in two tanks to pull the gate down.

The reason the soldiers could not open the gate was that there was a huge mound of corpses and dying people piled high against it. The SS had just recently left the camp. Locked everything up. No food. No water. Nothing. So these poor people tried to get out the gate and had died there.

And the poor GIs. These were battle-hardened troops. They had fought some of the bloodiest battles in Italy. But when they came into this camp…when they saw and smelled it… many of them ran back out and vomited. Hundreds and hundreds of rotting and mostly dead human beings, skeletons with skin on them. They had thrown themselves against the gate in a desperate attempt at freedom. To this day, over sixty years later, I cannot think of these poor souls dying in such a horrible way without completely breaking down.

⌒⌒⌒

During my weeks with the Americans in Eldena I met a young German woman, a Red Cross nurse, Ruth, who was quartered at the farm next to us, just a short walk away. She was a little bit older and had no children, but she had suffered as I had, having been beaten and raped by the Russians. We became friends. Ruth had a married sister in Dortmund in western Germany, not far from the Dutch border. Her sister had a husband and family and a home there. Ruth's goal was to get to Dortmund, because she believed she could live with her sister and start a new life.

Late one night I was in bed with Roland beside me, both of us sound asleep, when there was banging on my window. There was a nine o'clock curfew, and as I awoke from my deep sleep, my first thought was, oh, my God, the Russians are here again. But it wasn't the Russians. It was Tom Bates. "Maria, Maria, wake up. Open up. Right away. I need to speak to you."

Alarmed, I let him in. He burst in and quickly closed the door behind him.

"Maria, I've got some bad news," he said in a soft voice, "so, sit down and listen carefully."

I sank onto the bed, my chest tightening and adrenalin rising.

He looked down at me, grim-faced. "Maria, early tomorrow morning, we're pulling out, and they're sending us to Japan. The Russians are going to move into this area, and you know what that means. You have to get out. Now. You must leave at once.

You can't wait a minute. If they catch you…"

I was overwhelmed. I couldn't even move. Tom grabbed me by the shoulders and shook me. "Maria, you have to leave right away. Do you understand? You have to go. Now!"

"Yes, yes, I understand," I said, trying not to cry.

He went out to his jeep and came back with a big box filled with cartons of cigarettes, chocolates, and coffee. "Here, take this with you. Sorry I don't have much else for you, but this should help." My eyes filled with tears.

He started out the door. Then he turned back. "Maria, here's my address in the States." He handed me a piece of paper. "If you ever make it there, call me."

I was panic-stricken. "Get hold of yourself, Maria," I said out loud. "Think. Think." I knew that the Russians might catch me again. If they did, I would have to kill myself somehow, because if I did not, they would. And I would suffer horribly before I died. I looked down at Roland sleeping on the bed and shuddered. I didn't want to think about what would happen to him. Those thoughts goaded me into action. We had to leave and right this minute. But, how would I get out of Eldena?

Then, it came to me—the Red Cross. I knew that the Americans and the British respected Red Cross nurses, regardless of nationality. They treated them as their own. In other words they didn't rape Red Cross nurses, not that there were not isolated cases. And I thought of Ruth. She was a Red Cross nurse—and she had an extra uniform, and we were about the same size.

Quietly I left the house, walked over to the next farm, and tapped on Ruth's window. Like me, she was at first petrified. Finally, she let me in. With great urgency, I said, "Look, Ruth, I have something to tell you. It is a matter of life and death, yours and mine. I am going to tell you, but before I do, you have to pay me for it. This really is a matter of life and death."

"Pay you. How can I pay you? I have nothing. I don't have as much as you do. I own nothing."

"Yes, you do, Ruth. You have an extra Red Cross nurse's uniform. I want it, and not just to borrow it. I want it. You have to give it to me." I looked straight into her eyes.

She hesitated, "Well…"

"No, you have to decide this instant, right now. There is no time."

"Okay. Okay. I agree. Now, what is it?"

I told her everything Tom had told me. She was beside herself. "How are we going to live? How will we survive? What will we eat?"

"Don't worry. I have some things the Americans have given me. Let me change into your nurse's uniform, and we can leave."

Out behind the barn was a little cart with large wheels the size of bicycle wheels and a long tongue with a handle at the end. I took it and put the trading goods Tom had given me in the bottom, blankets on top of them, and Roland on top of the blankets. Ruth and I got on either side of the tongue and pulled it. We were very careful to hide the cigarettes, chocolates, and coffee, because if we had been caught with it, we could have been charged by the Americans for stealing American property.

About four o'clock in the morning, in the pitch black darkness, two tired nurses trudged down the road to the west. Roland had no idea what was going on. He started crying, and I managed to quiet him with pieces of chocolate.

We came to an American checkpoint. I had chills running

down my body, because at any moment they might catch us. I just knew the guard could smell the chocolate or the cigarettes or the coffee. If he found this contraband, we'd be arrested—and probably left with the Russians. Very curious, he stopped us. He could see our Red Cross uniforms, and I told him we were being reassigned to the hospital in Uelzen, a town about fifty miles away. I had no idea if there was a hospital in Uelzen, and, more importantly, I had no idea if the guard knew either. But, apparently, he did not. He let us pass without checking the contents of our stolen cart. We were on our way.

13

To Dortmund

The Elbe River was only about six miles away, but it was dark. Ruth and I stayed off the main roads, which was fortunate. Not long after we left Eldena, the Americans began pulling out, their trucks lumbering down the roads heading west. Close behind came the Russians. We were petrified.

We hid often, but we kept moving and finally got to the river a short time after daylight. There were no bridges in sight—except for a pontoon bridge farther upstream, which the Americans were using. It was guarded and we could not get near it. We stood on the riverbank discussing what to do, and Tata came to mind and his teaching me how to swim.

I was an excellent swimmer, thanks to him. I was such a klutz as a child, so uncoordinated. Tata had tried and tried to teach me to swim, without success. He bought me every conceivable floatation device there was, and I just could not get the hang of it.

But I trusted him totally, so he would put me on his back and swim out into the ocean. One summer in Split we swam quite far out, and suddenly he turned quickly and I slid off his back. "Swim!" he commanded, and I started flailing around and gasping—but I swam back on my own with him beside me. That was the way he was. He would always challenge me. I stood there on the riverbank and wondered what he was doing at that moment.

Ruth interrupted my thoughts. "What are we going to do, Maria?" she asked.

I believed that I could easily have swum across, but we could not even think about swimming, not with Roland, the cart, and all our contraband. There were not any Russians nearby, but we knew we had to get to the other side quickly. Other refugees were starting to arrive, too, and we had little time to spare.

We walked along the riverbank until we found a man with a boat. He was menacing, an older man, but big and strong enough to do anything he wanted with us. We approached him meekly and asked about getting across the river. He scowled. "What do you have to offer?" I gave him a carton of cigarettes. He kept his hand out, and I gave him some of our precious chocolates. Even with cigarettes and chocolates, he wasn't satisfied. We were a little hesitant to give him much else, because we didn't know what the future held for us. After some hesitation, Ruth pulled out a beautiful aquamarine stone she wore on a chain and offered that to him. He looked at it for some moments and finally said, "All right. Get in the boat."

To call this craft a boat was, perhaps, a flight of imagination. It was a rowboat about twelve or fifteen feet long, but it reminded me more of something that Huckleberry Finn would have used. It was old, leaky, unpainted, and rotten looking, and I expected it to fall apart at any moment. Water stood an inch deep in the bottom. I did not see how we could possibly get across the river in it.

With grave misgivings we climbed in, Ruth, Roland and I, and the old man. There was even room for our little cart. When we got in the boat, the old man was mumbling something about being sick and tired of all these damn women—he never stopped cursing us. I was afraid of what he would do to us, but what choice did we have?

When we were in mid-stream, we heard gunfire, and bullets started splattering the water all around us. Russian soldiers standing on the riverbank we had just left were shooting at us. They were howling and shouting and were probably drunk. They did not seem to care whether they hit us or not. It was just great fun to shoot at someone who was trying to escape, but for us out in the middle of this great wide river, it was terrifying.

Eventually, the Russians tired of shooting, and miraculously, the boat got to the far shore. We were safe on the American side. We jumped out of the boat, grabbed our cart, and hurried off, anxious to get away from the menacing boatman.

We began walking through a pretty area, not much ravaged by the war. At first there were no houses, but we soon came to a nice farmhouse on top of a slight hill. We knocked on the door, hoping to get some milk or something, anything to eat. We were also thinking that perhaps the owners would let us sleep in the barn. No one answered our knock. We tried again, but there was complete silence. We tried to open the door, but it would not budge. We went around the house to the back door and walked in. Russians had been there. At least from the destruction and vandalism, I assumed it had to have been Russians. The reason the front door would not open was because a whole family, five of them, had been shot, probably trying to get away and were piled up against the door. Hundreds of flies buzzed around the bodies. We did not stay.

As we headed west again, we could hear Russian voices off in the distance. I don't know what they were doing on this side of the Elbe, but lines between the various Allied forces didn't seem to be well defined at that time. Knowing the Russians were not too far away made us hurry all the more. We stayed off the main roads as much as possible and continued on toward Dortmund, over two hundred miles away.

Along the way we acquired eleven other refugees. I guess that, because we were wearing Red Cross nurse uniforms, they expected us to help them. I do not remember them all, but I do recall a German soldier who had lost a leg, his pregnant wife and two small children, and his aged parents. They, too, were running from the Russians. We had to help them. Ruth and I continued pulling the cart, the invalid soldier, his wife, his two children, and his parents all taking turns riding as we ponderously trudged down the road, our only clear destination, Dortmund. Of course, there was no room for Roland in the cart, so I had to carry him on my back. My legs and back throbbed with pain. My whole body screamed in agony. I remember thinking I am never going to survive this.

Once more everyone was always hungry, literally starving. We had to beg for food; I wasn't going to use our contraband except as a last resort. Because we were in an area occupied by Americans, and I was the only one who spoke English, I always had the onerous task of doing the begging. It was degrading. I don't know how many times I had to beg, but I do remember three incidents on that walk to Dortmund.

At one American camp the others in our group saw the sentry with his gun guarding the entrance. They were frightened. Guns meant shooting, so they stayed down on the road, and I went up to the soldier and humbly asked, "Please, sir, could you give us something to eat, anything. We have not eaten in days." He looked at me and down at our motley, ragged little group and said, "Just a minute." He left and came back shortly with a great big tomato juice can filled with scraps of food, no spoons or utensils, just the big can filled with food. I went back down to the group and we sat on the edge of the road and gobbled down everything in the can. The pregnant woman ate first, then the old people, injured man, and children. The rest of us took what was left over. Half-eaten pork chops, bits of vegetables, spaghetti, soggy bread pieces. We just rammed our hands in, pulled out what we could grab, and ate it. When we had devoured everything in the can, we walked on.

At another American camp the group stayed down on the road as usual, and I went up to beg for food. "Please, sir, may we have something to eat?" Even though I was wearing a Red Cross uniform and speaking English, the soldier pointed his rifle at me and snarled, "You goddamn Nazi whore. Get out of my sight before I kill you." I was devastated. I ran back down to the group in tears, totally humiliated.

We walked on. Of course, the two children and Roland cried, and the old people complained. Somehow, they felt that it was my fault when this soldier threatened me and said he was going to shoot me. They complained bitterly that Ruth and I were not taking good enough care of them. After all, we were nurses, weren't we? We had an obligation.

Several days later we came to another American camp, and an older man, an officer, happened to be at the gate with the sentry and some others. He looked at me kindly, like he had a soul. Again I asked, "Please, sir, could you give us something to eat?"

He gazed down at our group and asked, "Who are these people?"

I explained our circumstances, how Ruth and I had met in Eldena and how we had collected the other refugees and that we were making our way to Dortmund. "We don't really know them. We're just trying to help them."

He looked at me with sad eyes. "I have a daughter about your age. Wait a minute."

He walked back into the camp with one of the soldiers who had been standing there and returned a short time later—with a wagon and an old horse and food. I could not believe it. My heart was in my throat and tears in my eyes. "Here, we can't use these," he said, "and I'm sure you can. This old horse is in pretty good shape and should get you to Dortmund."

"Oh, thank you, sir. Thank you, thank you." Exhilarated, I led the horse down the hill to our group as the American officer stood there smiling.

We gorged ourselves right there by the road. Everyone was laughing and joking. After we had eaten our fill, we loaded all our treasures on the wagon and started down the road. The legless soldier, his family, and Roland all rode in the wagon. Ruth, I, and some of the others still had to walk, but at least we were not pulling the cart, which we had left beside the road at the camp. And it was fortunate that I didn't have to carry Roland, since my feet had no feeling left in them.

Two nights later we stopped in a little meadow just off the road. A stream gurgled alongside. We always tried to spend the night near water, so that we could have something to drink and so that Ruth and I could wash our white Red Cross aprons. This night, still somewhat feeling the euphoria of our good fortune, and still having food given to us by the American officer, we ate a good meal and lay down to sleep, the nearby stream singing us a sweet lullaby.

The next morning when we woke up, everything was gone: the refugees, the horse, the wagon, the food, everything we had, all gone. Just Ruth and Roland and I lying out in that little meadow. These eleven people, for whom we had done so much, whom we had cared for and fed, had stolen everything and left us. What were we going to do? What would we eat? Ruth and I sat there and sobbed.

Finally, we got ourselves together and started walking again, Roland on my back, without even our little cart. We no longer had any cigarettes or chocolate or anything else to trade for food, but we vowed to each other that we were going to make it to Dortmund. I was the English speaker and could still beg for food.

Eventually we came upon a large field of cabbages. Men with shotguns were guarding it, but we waited until after dark, and I slowly crawled into the field, trying to be as quiet as possible, and grabbed one cabbage. That was what we had to eat for the next week. I had to chew the leaves to soften them before I put them in Roland's mouth, but at least he had some nourishment.

❧❧

Then one day our luck changed. A British truck came by and

picked us up. The British really respected nurses, even German nurses. They did not have anything to eat, but several miles down the road, they pulled into an Allied field hospital. We went inside and offered our medical services. When the hospital administrator asked us what sort of nurses we were, Ruth said she was an OR nurse and I told them I worked in the delivery room.

"Well, you can stay," they said to Ruth, "but we don't need you"—meaning me.

"Oh, no," we said. "We're together. Either we both stay or we both go."

I told them that I was very good in the kitchen. Perhaps I was fibbing a bit, but I had learned a good deal about cooking during my time in Laaslich, so we both got to stay. The staff did not allow Ruth to do really important things in the OR, because she was German, but she worked hard, cleaning floors, emptying bed pans, and changing linens. The cooks didn't allow me to do a lot of cooking either, but I earned my keep, washing dishes.

They fed us, of course, but having starved for weeks and months and even years, we were both permanently hungry. Because I was in the kitchen, I had the opportunity to steal food, which I did as often as I could. Little pats of butter, pieces of bread, milk, a cookie a patient had not eaten—these I would take to our room in the cellar and share with Ruth. I'm not very proud of that now, but at the time it didn't seem so bad.

Life in that little field hospital was good for us, but we had no intention of remaining. Our goal was Dortmund. If we could get to Dortmund, we could start a new life. Everything would be better. This nightmare would be over for us. So we decided after a few weeks in the hospital that it was time to leave. We planned to start walking again in the middle of the night after Ruth and I had gotten off work and rested for a few hours. We had not said anything to the hospital staff, of course.

That day I managed to steal a bowl of sour milk, which I left for Ruth on the window sill in our room. Sour milk probably does not sound very appetizing, but when you are starved as we were, it is actually very tasty. When Ruth got off work, and I gave her the bowl of sour milk, she drank it down all at once. Later she had diarrhea so badly that we had to delay our departure for several days. When Ruth had recovered we finally did leave and we did reach Dortmund, our goal, our chance to start a new life.

Dortmund was a huge pile of rubble. Only a few streets had been cleared, but nothing was recognizable. Ruth was distraught. She could not find her sister's house or even her street. She had no idea whether her sister and her family were alive or dead, and if they were alive, where they might be.

While we were looking for Ruth's sister, we met a young man standing in the middle of a path cleared between piles of rubble and crying. He could not find his wife and child and believed that they were buried under all that debris. He was probably right. Like so many thousands of people, Jews and non-Jews, Germans and non-Germans, this man's family and Ruth's sister's family simply had disappeared with no trace.

Many people in western Germany went east because of rumors that things were better there, and many in the east went west for the same reason. That is why so many refugees were wandering around the country. It was completely illogical, but that was the mentality. People were so frantic to stay alive, to find any shred of the past, they would believe anything. That was

CROSSING THE ELDE BRIDGE

Ruth and I, too.

Now that our dream of Dortmund had been shattered, we had to come up with another plan. We met some other refugees who said that things were better in France, about one hundred seventy miles to the south. Rumor had it that a monastery just across the border was taking care of refugees. What could we lose? We could not stay in the charred ruins of what had been Dortmund, so the three of us, Ruth, Roland, and I, got back on the road and started walking south following another illusion.

14

Disaster Strikes

Rain fell without ceasing, which made walking wretched. Occasionally, we might get a ride on an American or British Army truck, but most of the time we simply plodded south, begging or stealing food wherever we could and hoping for the day we would reach France.

Everything was gray, the fields and roads and sky. The whole world had been destroyed and was covered with mud, miles and miles of dirty gray muck. Fighting in this area, obviously, had been intense, because no trees stood, few buildings even, and most of those at least partially destroyed. And there were bomb craters everywhere. Sometimes a road ended at a huge bomb crater, and we had to work our way around it or climb down into it and out again. And often times unexploded bombs would detonate and kill or injure dozens of people around it. Everything everywhere stank of urine and decay. Little picturesque villages, beautiful before the war, were filled with ruined houses, streets impassable because of the debris, rotting corpses, and bomb craters.

CROSSING THE ELDE BRIDGE

Demoralized, starving, ill-clothed, dirty, we trudged on, thinking only of getting to the monastery where we could eat and bathe and be safe. We were on the very edge of total collapse. Without exception everyone we encountered was miserable, dressed in filthy rags and half-starved. I did not meet a single human being who did not stink, because there was no soap and no running water. We had no clean underwear; many people did not have any underwear. If you had a piece of bread, you devoured it like an animal, because if you did not, someone would take it from you. And if you had to relieve yourself, you hid behind a skimpy bush along the road or behind a building that was now in ruins. Life was a nightmare.

And being with hordes of refugees wandering aimlessly, you did not know what you were exposing yourself to. There were all kinds of people traveling on the road, criminals, lunatics, people who had absolutely nothing to live for. The Allies were attempting to restore order. They had checkpoints and posts, and they patrolled the roads in jeeps, but for the masses, especially in those early months at the end of the war, anarchy was almost absolute. If you met someone who had a coat, why not just kill him and take the coat? And beneath the coat, he probably wore a pair of pants and a shirt which might be traded for a couple of eggs or a pack of cigarettes. There was very little risk in killing someone, because there were no German police, and the Allies never got too upset about a dead German body.

We had been riding in a British truck and at one point the driver had to turn off, so he stopped to let us out. Just down the road were some refugees gathered in a bomb crater. We joined the group. Roland was crying because he was hungry. A nice German soldier, a sub-lieutenant, came over and gave a piece of cookie to Roland, who devoured it and fell immediately to sleep. The young man stayed there talking to us, and he seemed so nice. At this point, I feared most males, but I felt secure with him. We talked and talked. I told him about my parents and grandmother and husband and my concerns for them. He seemed genuinely interested. Finally, as dusk began to fall, people spread out a bit and things quieted down. The young man left, and I sat there beginning to doze off with Roland asleep beside me.

When I opened my eyes the German sub-lieutenant had reappeared and he was unbuttoning his fly. I suppose I should have expected it, but I did not. I can still see those buttons and those hands. Even worse was that not far away there were others lying around copulating, many of them willingly. It was as if people were trying to hang on to life in the midst of all this devastation. Even so, I cursed myself for trusting another man.

The rest of that trip was just endless walking, the roads crowded with people of all sizes, ages, civilians, soldiers, different nationalities. God knows where they came from and where they were going, but everybody was moving somewhere, because all the cities in western Germany, the industrial part of Germany, had been destroyed, and there was simply no place to live.

❧

Finally, after I do not know how many days of walking, hitching rides with the Americans and British, and stealing food or begging for it, we reached France, somewhere around Saarbrucken. As I look at a map today, it is about 170 miles straight-line distance from Dortmund to Saarbrucken and perhaps 200 miles by road. The border between France and Germany was rather porous then because of the millions of refugees wandering around, and it was easy to get across. We headed for the monastery, our spirits rising with every step.

Almost as soon as we arrived, however, our hopes again were dashed. The monastery was so crowded there was no place for us to stay. Perhaps the brothers were overwhelmed, but they certainly did not act Christian toward us or anyone else, even going so far as to hit us if we were not prompt in following their directions. The food they gave us was watered-down gruel, with almost no nutritional value and almost inedible. In less than twenty-four hours Ruth and I decided we would rather suffer in Germany than in that horrible place. At least we had some kind of connection, and we knew the country.

We headed back across the border and decided to go to Osnabruck, which was north of Dortmund and about three hundred miles away. We were hardened to the rigors of wandering refugees, adept at sensing trouble, hitching rides, especially with the British, and at getting at least enough food to stay alive. We were always on the edge of complete exhaustion, and I had the additional burden of carrying Roland, but we just kept on moving.

☙❧

After several weeks on the road at summer's end, the three of us arrived at the Osnabruck train station, Ruth and I still wearing our Red Cross nurses' uniforms. Much to our delight the first thing we saw was a train full of German POWs, leaning out the windows. And walking along the platform beside the train were… Red Cross nurses in crisp, clean uniforms with baskets of sandwiches, which they were passing out to the men. Our uniforms were in tatters and we stunk to high heaven, but we were dressed as Red Cross nurses, so we approached the women and offered to help.

Of course, they took one look at us and said no thank you, they didn't need our help. We pestered them a little. Ruth showed them her Red Cross identification, which miraculously she still had, and I told them mine had been lost. Finally, they gave us both baskets of sandwiches and directed us toward the back of the train, out of the way.

My uniform was so filthy. I was embarrassed at first, but then I became defiant. I started hating those nurses, so prim and proper in their starched caps, pressed uniforms, and their snow-white aprons. What we had gone through, we couldn't have been any different. Who were they to judge us?

As we walked back toward the end of the train, we ate our share of sandwiches. By then Roland was crying, and I was still upset by the way we had been treated. When we got to the last car we started handing out sandwiches to the soldiers hanging out the windows, and a man who reminded me a little of Jurgen looked at me and said, "Sister, Sister (nurses and nuns were addressed as *Schwester*, Sister), you don't look like a sister to me. You look like a whore."

That was the final straw and I burst into tears. I was so overwhelmed by all that had happened to me, and this man's words ripped into me. Nausea overcame me. I started shaking, staggering. Someone grabbed Roland and helped Ruth get into me into the caboose. I remember lying on a bench there and the conductor putting his coat over me, because I was shivering uncontrollably.

The next thing I remember was waking up in a hospital.

15

More Trials

I was in a hospital, yes, but I was not in a bed. I was standing in a room holding the hand of a woman I had never seen before in my life, and I was wearing a crisp, clean nurse's uniform. The woman was saying, "Sister, Sister, you saved my life. I never could have had this baby without you." Apparently, I had been working in the hospital delivery room. As soon as I could, I patted her hand, congratulated her on a fine baby, and left the room. I could not remember exactly where I was or who this woman was, but vague memories flashed through my mind, and as I was leaving the room I suddenly realized that I had a child. Where was my child? I went to the nurses' station and approached one of the nurses who had a kindly face.

By talking to her I was able to reconstruct what had happened to me. I had collapsed completely at the railroad station in Osnabruck. The combination of eating those Red Cross sandwiches, the first decent food we had had in days, and the German soldier's harangue had brought me to the breaking point.

CROSSING THE ELDE BRIDGE

I was so physically and mentally exhausted that I had a nervous breakdown with resulting amnesia. The nurse told me that after the train conductor and Ruth had gotten me into the caboose, the train had gone to Holland, and that is where I had ended up. The conductor had taken Roland and me to a hospital in Enschede and had left us there. I don't know how long Ruth stayed with me, but by the time I regained my memory, she was gone. I never blamed her; she had her own life to live, and I certainly did not expect her to saddle herself with a sickly woman and a child. I never saw her again, but I often wonder what happened to her, and I will never forget her friendship.

I do not remember how long I was unconscious, but at some point I came to and told the Enschede hospital staff the same thing Ruth and I had been telling every hospital we passed. I was a Red Cross nurse, and I worked in Maternity. I suppose I finally convinced them, and they gave me a new uniform and let me help in the Maternity Ward. I do not remember any of this, but I assume that is what happened.

I asked the nurse where my child was. She took me by the hand and led me to the room where the nurses congregated and ate. It was a large, comfortable, warm room. In the middle was a large box, and there sat Roland, fat and clean and happy, gurgling "rah, rah, rah." The nursing staff had taken very good care of him, spoiled him, and I almost cried to see him so healthy and happy.

॰॰॰

We were there two or three weeks after I regained my memory. Winter was not far away, and I became anxious to get back into Germany. The staff was wonderful, but I knew we could not stay indefinitely. I did not know where we would go, however. The only family I had was in Laaslich, which probably was controlled by the Russians. There was a good chance all my relatives had been killed. Besides, I dreaded going back amongst the Russians. I was petrified just thinking about it.

Then I remembered the Reimers, the nice couple with whom Jurgen and I had stayed briefly when he was stationed at the air base in Quickborn north of Hamburg. It was less than two hundred miles away. The British occupied that part of the country, and from what I had heard most of the towns up there, except for Hamburg, had not been so devastated by the war. So I decided we would head to Quickborn. With the blessings of the hospital staff, we departed. They had provided me winter clothes for Roland, a heavy gray coat for me, some food, and even a little money.

Again I started walking, Roland on my back. The days were not bad, although it did rain occasionally. Nights were cold, and we seldom found much shelter. Most of the time we simply left the road and huddled under trees. I had long before learned that making a big pile of leaves and burrowing into the middle of the pile was a good way to stay warm, and the coat the hospital staff had given me was big enough to cover both Roland and me.

Each day, though, I grew weaker, and Roland's constant whimpering further eroded my strength and my spirit. Finally, after several days on the road I was so exhausted that I couldn't go on. We came to a small town, I don't remember the name of it, and I found an orphanage on the main street. An idea struck me, and I went inside.

As soon as I entered, the supervisor stopped me. "I'm sorry. Only orphans are allowed here."

CROSSING THE ELDE BRIDGE

I decided to tell the man what he wanted to hear. "Yes, yes, I know, but this child is an orphan. His mother is dead. I'm his aunt. Couldn't I leave him here for two days? I am looking for his grandparents who lived here before the war. I promise I'll come back as soon as I find them, and if I cannot find them, I will fetch him. Please, sir.'

He relented. "Well, two days then, only two."

"I promise. He is my sister's son, and I won't abandon him." Then I left. Of course, I was not looking for any grandparents. I was looking for some respite, which I soon found in a bombed-out building. There was one wall left and a staircase. Underneath it was quite cozy, and I had my big warm coat. I crawled in out of the cold and wind and made myself comfortable. By then it was late afternoon, and I soon fell asleep. I did not awaken until late the next day. I had to relieve myself, which I did behind the wall of the building. Then I climbed back into my cubby hole and was soon asleep. I did not wake up until the next morning. When I went to retrieve Roland, the supervisor at the orphanage was much relieved to see me, and Roland clapped his little hands and reached out for me, gurgling happily.

♦

When we left the town, our luck changed. We were able to travel more quickly, mostly because of the occasional rides from the British, and arrived in Quickborn in a matter of days. I was overjoyed.

The town had hardly been touched by the war, at least physically. With a happy heart and Roland in my arms I walked up the street to the Reimers' house. Werner answered my knock and opened the door. Surprise and delight spread across his face.

"It's Maria Kohler," he shouted over his shoulder, and welcomed me with open arms. Lotte rushed to the door and threw her arms around me, too. At last, I thought, I have found a safe haven. I was sorely disappointed.

We talked for a long time catching up on each other's lives and what had happened to us over the last years. They invited me to eat and to stay with them. When we sat down for the meal, I was quite surprised at the food. There were large portions, and it was very good. "You seem to have fared well," I said, just making conversation.

"Well, yes, we have, Maria," Werner replied. "And with you here, things can be even better."

I was puzzled. "What do you mean, Werner?"

He looked at me for a moment. Lotte just stared down at her food. She was not smiling any longer. "Yes, you see," he said, "we live so well because of the Tommies up on the hill."

"The Tommies, the British?"

"Yes, of course. I make arrangements, and they come down here to spend a little time with Lotte. With you here, we can double what we make. One blond and one brunette. You can start tomorrow. It's not so bad, and at least we don't starve. In fact, we're living pretty well, as you can see. You'll get used to it."

"What? You want me to be a prostitute?" I was stunned.

He grasped my arm. "You have to do it, Maria. There's no other way."

I was shocked and outraged. "No, I won't. I will not be a whore for you." I jumped up, grabbing Roland, and raced out of the house.

As I ran down the street I remembered that as I came in at

the edge of town, I had seen a forest and some small cabins, which were probably weekend lodges. That's where we headed. Shivering with cold, we had to find shelter. When we arrived in the forest, I searched for a cabin which was unlocked and was lucky enough to find one. It was small, just one room, perhaps twelve feet square, but it had a bed, a table, two chairs, a cabinet—and a stove. And there was wood right outside. I brought some in, found paper and matches, and started a fire. We would be warm that night. I put paper and wood into the stove and lit it. Almost immediately thick, noxious smoke started pouring out. The wood was wet, and the flue may have been jammed. Roland was asleep on the bed already, but I hurriedly took him out because we could have died from that smoke.

I had begun to feel ill, and I really did not want to leave, but I knew we couldn't stay in the smoke-filled cabin. So I took Roland, crying, and carried him back into Quickborn. I was feeling worse all the time, vomiting a few times on the way. And it was getting colder as night drew near. I was desperate.

When we got back into town I saw a doctor's sign and went there. I knew I was very sick, and by now I had terrible diarrhea. The doctor looked me over briefly, shook his head sadly, and told me I had typhoid. "I can't give you any medicine, because I don't have any, not even to help you with your diarrhea. If you can find some rice, I suppose that will help, but I have nothing to give you."

I was dismayed. "Doctor," I asked. "Where can I get rice? There is almost nothing here or any place in the country to eat."

He pointed out the window and said, "See that hill up there? That's where the Tommies are." He pushed my hair away from my face and said, "You know, if you fix yourself up a little bit, you're not half-bad looking. You could get anything you want from the Tommies." With that he dismissed me, and I walked down the two or three steps of his building and started across the cobblestone square clutching Roland tightly to me. It was snowing.

The cobblestones seemed to be shifting, and I got dizzier and dizzier. I fell to my knees thinking I was dying. I lost consciousness. When I awoke and opened my eyes, I was lying on a cot and looking into the wrinkled face of a very old woman sitting in a rickety chair nearby. She was holding Roland, who was placidly sleeping. I looked around me and saw that I was in what I can only describe as a tiny hut.

When the old woman saw that I was awake she leaned forward and in a kindly voice asked, "Are you feeling better, child?" I nodded. She introduced herself as Anna and then told me what had happened. She had passed by my unconscious body and my screaming, terrified child in the snowy square and had somehow managed to carry us to her little hut, I think probably with someone's help. She had undressed me, cleaned me, and washed my clothes. She had also cleaned up Roland and put him in clean clothes. When I woke up I was wearing one of her old shapeless shifts, probably the only thing she had besides what she was wearing herself.

And incredibly, she fed me eggs and rice and nursed me back to health. I do not know where or how she obtained the food, but somehow, she took care of us for weeks.

16

A Miracle

I do not remember exactly how long we stayed with Anna, but one day she came in and with a faltering voice told me that Roland and I would have to leave, because her son was coming home. She was very sorry, but there just was not room. I understood perfectly. After all, she had nursed me back to health and taken care of my child for I did not know how long and I am sure at great deprivation. I had nothing to repay her with except my eternal gratitude.

"But," she said, "don't worry. I know a man not far from here whose wife died a few months ago, and he needs a housekeeper. I have already talked to him, and you can go there." I was overcome by her caring and generosity.

Anna went with us to show me the way. The man, Herr Erdrich, lived a good way out of town on the moors. I was still so weak I could hardly walk, but Anna carried Roland. After what seemed like several hours of walking we finally arrived at a small house and were greeted by a short, stocky, elderly man with a warm smile. He seemed genuinely happy to see us.

Herr Erdrich harvested peat for fuel. The winter weather in that area was brutal, not only because of the cold but also because of the bitter wind. The moors were flat and nearly treeless, and the wind howled uninterrupted from the North Sea all the way across the peninsula. Herr Erdrich's house consisted of a bedroom, kitchen, parlor, and a basement, filled with shelf after shelf of all sorts of canned goods, which his wife had put up in previous years.

Yes, he could use a housekeeper. I was to sleep in the kitchen on a cot and Roland in a box on the kitchen floor. I had to do the cooking, cleaning, and laundry—and I was welcome to eat whatever I wanted from the larder in the cellar. Anna must have told him how starved I had been.

Cooking and cleaning were not a problem. I shook out Herr Erdrich's bedding every day and aired it, swept out the entire house, washed and dried the dishes, and scrubbed the kitchen from top to bottom. Laundry was a different story. Working in the peat fields was hard, dirty work, and people at that time did not change their clothes every day. They did not have much extra clothing, so when clothes did get washed they were absolutely filthy. In fact, Herr Erdrich would go weeks wearing the same underwear and outer clothing.

Additionally, in the country, people hardly ever took a bath, especially in winter. Every house had a well with a pump outside. There was no running water in most houses. People would go to the pump in the morning to wash their faces, hands, and arms and do the same in the evening before they came in. This added to the dirtiness of their clothing.

I had to do the washing outside in the bitter cold and unending

A MIRACLE

wind; there was no room in the house. I knelt or squatted before a big tub, scrubbing on a washboard, using the same kind of foul-smelling, homemade lye soap that our poor washerwoman in Vienna had used on the steps of our house so many years ago. As a child I often watched her at work, wondering how she could stand to have her hands covered with that awful soap all day long. Now, my own hands were cracked and bleeding just like hers.

I would scrub and scrub Herr Erdrich's clothes, black from peat and reeking with body odor. When I had scrubbed and rinsed the soap from the sheets or his shirts or underwear or other clothing, I would hang them on the clothes line. They would be frozen in minutes. And his clothes were heavy homespun. It was difficult to manage more than one piece at a time. As I was able, I would take individual pieces and hang them up in the kitchen during the day to dry by the fire, but there was not enough room for everything, so drying took several days.

Herr Erdrich arose every morning at four. He was very thoughtful and told me I did not have to get up then, but he would come into the kitchen, get the fire going, and make his coffee. That is all he would have, and maybe a piece of bread, before he went out to work. Later, he returned for his morning meal. I was grateful not to have to get up that early because of the biting cold. The house was very primitive with no insulation and many cracks in the walls. The wind roared right through them.

Meals tended to be monotonous, if hot and filling. We had a few chickens, but otherwise very little meat. We did have lots of canned vegetables and fruits, so I most often made stews, even for breakfast. Herr Erdrich always praised my cooking, but I know it was not that good. He was being kind.

On Sunday Herr Erdrich went to church. He was a Lutheran.

He had one suit, which he would put on with a clean shirt and trot off into the snow and wind. He asked me if I would like to go, and out of respect, even though I had been raised Catholic, I did. I actually enjoyed myself. We would walk along and Herr Erdrich would carry Roland. In church they sang many hymns, and I joined right in. Church was a bright spot in my drab existence.

One day after we had been on the moors a few months, we were walking back from church and Herr Erdrich said, "You know, I'm so glad that you sing with us, because you have a beautiful voice."

"Thank you," I said.

He was silent for a few minutes as we bent into the wind and crunched through the snow. Then he said, "You really keep the house very nice and you cook so well."

"Thank you," I said again.

Silence once more. "Well, as you know, I'm a widower, and I would like to marry you."

I blanched. I said, "Well, I like you very much, but I cannot marry you. I am already married." Inwardly I was dying. Did I want to spend the rest of my life scrubbing floors and doing laundry out on the moors? You could not see another house anywhere, and I never saw another human being except Herr Erdrich and Roland for days and days. Could I really endure life with this man? What about my husband—the man I really loved?

I pondered all of this. Herr Erdrich had been very kind to Roland and me, and he had never tried to touch me or even say anything inappropriate, but I distrusted men in general after everything that had happened to me. I thought that somehow I had to leave. I had to get back to Laaslich.

It was the only point of reference I had left. Berlin was utterly destroyed, and Laaslich may have been too, but I could not know for certain. I had to find out if my husband, my in-laws, my parents and grandmother were alive or dead. In the Russian area or not, Laaslich continued to call to me. For weeks these things hung heavily on my heart and mind.

∽∞∾

One day in late winter I was standing at the stove in the kitchen looking out the window, and I saw a figure coming across the moor. Who is that, I wondered. It was too early for Herr Erdrich, and besides, this person did not walk the same way as he. As the figure came nearer, I recognized him. I was dumbstruck.

It was Willy, my husband's cousin, and my good friend in Laaslich! I screamed, ran out calling his name, and threw my arms around him. In the howling wind we stood there staring at each other in disbelief, in tears.

After our shocked and joyful reunion, Willy and I finally came into the house and over a hot cup of coffee we began to talk. He had been taken as a POW to a camp in Denmark, where he had been living like a king. They had given him food and even chocolates, and everything had been very lax. One day he noticed that some of his fellow prisoners casually walked out of the camp and never came back. Nobody ever said anything about it. They did not run or sneak out. They strolled away from the camp, so Willy thought, why not?

As it turned out, Herr Erdrich's house was not far from the POW camp and more or less on a straight line to Laaslich about ninety miles away. Willy was walking across the moor and saw this little house. He had plenty of food but nothing to drink, so he came to the house to ask for some water. It was a miracle.

CROSSING THE ELDE BRIDGE

When Herr Erdrich returned from the peat fields, I told him what had happened. This was my cousin, my husband's cousin, on his way back home. And Herr Erdrich said, "Yes, of course, you must go with him." But I could tell that he really did not mean it. I knew he would be very lonely when we left, and I knew that I would miss him, too.

Herr Erdrich went into the cellar and came back up with a ham and all sorts of food and even produced a bottle of schnapps. That night we had a feast. After supper, he excused himself and went to bed. Willy and I sat in the kitchen and in muffled voices talked half the night away. I was too excited to sleep. The next day I would be going home.

17

Return to Laaslich

The next morning we prepared to leave. Herr Erdrich didn't go to the peat fields that day; he stayed at the house to see us off. Willy knew the country well and described the route we would be taking, crossing this and that river, and moving through a large forest. And he pointed out that we would probably encounter Russians. "Don't worry," Willy said. "We'll make you as repugnant-looking and smelling as possible."

Under Willy's instructions I smeared chicken droppings on my clothes and in my hair and rubbed dirt all over my body. I also smeared raspberry juice in my underwear as if I were having my period. If that did not stop the Russians from attacking me, Willy instructed me to say that I had syphilis. Sometimes they would kick you and scream at you but most often would leave you alone, although occasionally one would say, "Ah, syphilis good," and rape you anyway. Still, it was safer to take these precautions, and I took every one of them.

Willy was wearing a heavy SS coat—he wasn't SS—that he had

picked up in the POW camp, so I cut the insignia off and burned it in the kitchen stove. At that point, if anyone had suspected that he was SS they would have stoned him or shot him.

After another hearty meal, we were ready to leave. I gave Herr Erdrich my most heart-felt thanks and kissed him on the cheek. In return he gave us a large sack of food and his blessing. I bundled Roland up against the cold, Willy hoisted him on his back, and we started across the moors, headed for Laaslich. Herr Erdrich stood at the door and waved goodbye to us. He was smiling, but I could see the sadness in his eyes.

It was late winter, still freezing, and we walked for days. I wasn't all that hardy, and I stunk so badly I could hardly stand myself, but knowing that every step was a step closer to Laaslich, I carried on. One day as we entered a forested area we came to a meadow and saw a young Russian soldier walking up and down, trying to stay warm. I told Willy that I was his crazy aunt and to follow my lead. "Whatever you do, do not act surprised. I will handle this."

When we got closer I started hopping toward the soldier and yelling, "My little dove, my little dove, my little dove." I went right up to him, screeching "My little dove, my little dove," and jumped on him. He pushed me away and cursed at me. I continued jumping on him and pulling his ears. He kept trying to get away from me. Finally, Willy grabbed me and apologized to the soldier. "She's my aunt. I'm sorry. She's old and crazy." He dragged me off, apologizing the whole time, and we ran into the woods.

As we ran we did not know if the soldier would shoot us or not. I had seen Russian soldiers who were so sweet to little children and then, in an instant, shoot the mother. The young Russian must have been in a good mood that day and had taken pity on this poor German soldier who carried his child on his back and had to take care of his crazy, stinking old aunt. He did not shoot us.

We kept moving. At night Willy would build a small fire and make us a shelter of tree branches and brush with a pile of leaves for a bed, and we would huddle together and stay as warm as we could. Poor Roland was getting sick. He just lay in my arms whimpering and shivering. I kept him under my coat next to my body to keep him as warm as I could, but the weather was brutal. If we were lucky we would find a barn or sometimes an abandoned house where we could get out of the wind, but most often we spent the nights in the open and just suffered through until morning.

Eventually, we came to the Schaale River. The ice was too thin to walk across, and we could not find a boat, so we stayed there for several days. We ran out of food, but the one good thing was that we were only about fifty miles away from home. All three of us were worn down and exhausted, even Willy, but he still went out every day looking for food and a way to get across the river. One day he returned exuberant. He had found a bridge just a couple of miles downstream, and in spite of our weakened condition, we hurried down to it. And soon after we crossed the bridge and went on our way, we came across train tracks! And a train running on them! We managed to get on the train and well before nightfall we jumped off, a short distance from Laaslich.

It was just before dark on a late winter's day when Willy, still carrying Roland, and I trudged down a back road of Laaslich and into the farmyard behind the house. Mariechen happened to be standing at the kitchen window and saw us as we approached. We could hear her scream, as she and Tante Grete came rushing outside. We all stood there, Mariechen, Tante Grete, Willy, and I, motionless, stunned by the realization that we were finally home.

Mariechen came slowly up to me, her eyes welling with tears, and said softly, "Oh, my dear, what you must have gone through." I reached out for her but collapsed on the spot. By then, Erwin, who had earlier come to Laaslich, had come out of the house with Grandmother. He and Willy carried me inside. Mariechen and Tante Grete removed my clothes and bathed me as best they could, then put me to bed, where I remained for several weeks. Roland and Willy, too, were sick in bed for some time.

Because I was so ill, they had put Roland and me in a bed in the living room of the *altenteil* where the stove was located; they were not able to heat the whole house because of the lack of coal and the meager supply of wood. Erwin, the only man around, was in his seventies and not able to chop very much wood in a day. Still, I was so grateful to lie there in a real bed under a real roof, feeling secure. Roland and I were safe with people who loved us. That was more than enough.

❧

As I lay in bed those first few weeks, I became very depressed. With all that had happened to me the depth of pain and disgust and sadness and the desire not to be in this world anymore overwhelmed me. I prayed that God would let me die. What was there to live for? Did I ever have any reason to imagine that I would ever again live like a normal human being? Everything I had known in the past months and years had been destroyed, buildings, cities, roads, the whole society and the culture, everything in ruins. There was nothing but destruction and corruption and greed.

RETURN TO LAASLICH

What existed in my childhood was gone forever, and I knew it because of all the stories I had heard and because of all that I had seen and experienced myself. And even if places were not destroyed, but only abandoned, they were not empty for an hour before hordes of homeless refugees moved in. And I had no idea if my husband, my parents, or my grandmother were still alive. Most probably they were all dead, and these people were the only family I had left.

In the days to come we learned the fate of Willy's family and of the farm. The people had been brutalized. Uncle Otto had been dragged away by the Russians. We learned many years later that he had been thrown into a Russian POW camp and had starved to death. Mariechen and Tante Grete in their seventies and eighties had both been raped. Even old Mrs. Kappel, the midwife, had been badly abused. In fact, all the women in Laaslich had been raped and beaten. Many people had simply disappeared.

The farm had fared little better. The buildings were all intact, but the Russians had destroyed everything else. They had killed all the animals and removed everything worth taking. Now there was nothing but a few potatoes and rutabagas. There was nothing substantial, no meat. None of the things people desperately needed. If anyone ever found a chicken, it was cause for celebration, very, very special. The women could not do any laundry, because the Russians had stolen the big tubs they had used. They did the best they could to wash clothes in the sink in the house, but sheets stayed dirty. They were aired out when weather permitted, but they were never washed for months and months.

As I got better I finally was able to get out of bed and help out a little, and my depression began to lift. The more I was able to move about, the more I came to realize how desperate was the situation on the farm. Even though I was family, I was a tremendous burden on them all. I finally decided that I had to leave.

What I needed was to go to Berlin. If I stayed in Laaslich I would continue to be another mouth to feed. And I would never find out what happened to my husband, my parents, and my grandmother. With my language abilities I could be useful to the Allies. I needed to get to Berlin and find a job where I had some possibility of discovering if they were alive. Going to Berlin meant that I would have to leave Roland behind, but I knew Mariechen could take better care of him than I could by myself as a single working mother. And Mariechen, especially, encouraged me to go. I was sick at heart to leave Roland, but I had no choice, so that is what I did.

18

Back to Berlin

Fortunately, the train that had brought Willy and me to Laaslich also ran to Berlin, one of the few trains in service then. Conditions in the city appalled me. Huge piles of rubble lay everywhere. Most streets were filled with mountains of debris. Most buildings were demolished, an occasional wall rising up out of the rubble like a ghost from a grave. People were living just about anywhere they could find some kind of shelter, many of them like cockroaches in the dark, dank basements that had survived the Allied bombing.

Still, there were signs of life stirring amid the devastation. Reconstruction had already started. Crews, mostly American and British, were clearing the rubble from the streets. Others worked to restore the subway, the *Ubahn*, and the elevated train system, the *Esbahn*. And individuals, too, were at work. I saw whole families from small children who could barely walk to ancient grandparents, working together to clear the ruins of their homes, even squatting there together to scrape mortar off individual bricks and clean them for eventual rebuilding. It was moving to see this resilience amidst all the chaos.

And there was chaos. The Allies and the new German government that was slowly being reestablished worked valiantly at restoring and maintaining order, but crime was rampant. The city's infrastructure had been totally destroyed, and there was very little government to organize and control rebuilding efforts. Enormous masses of people still roamed the country and especially Berlin. All those hundreds of thousands of people from East Prussia who left everything to run from the Russians had no place to go except to the west. And then there were thousands of Germans who had been displaced by the war. Many of these people came to Berlin, just as I did.

I returned to the Kohlers' old neighborhood and found some of their friends. Through them I was able to obtain a room in what had been their apartment. It had been a beautiful apartment, much like the Kohlers', but had been bombed out. At the time the government required those with houses or apartments to take in as many refugees as they could hold. They assigned space, not by square meters, but by cubic meters, so people were packed into whatever abodes existed. Part of this apartment had been destroyed, but part was in fairly good shape. One family occupied what had been the living room and two other families the two intact bedrooms. I was assigned a tiny room beneath the stairs. At one time it might have been a servant's room or a storage area. It was so small there was barely room for a cot, but it did have a window, and I could look down on the street. The bathrooms had all been destroyed, so we just had to make do the best we could, wherever we could.

BACK TO BERLIN

With my language skills I got a job as a liaison working with the various Occupation Forces, which, to my intense dissatisfaction, included the Russians. Just being around them made my skin crawl. Otherwise, the work was incredibly interesting. I got to travel around, and, most importantly, I worked with many different agencies which gave me contacts and inside information in my search for my husband, parents, and grandmother. But I also learned horrible things, especially about the Russians, which intensified my profound fear of them.

As an example, there was a doctor from one of the Baltic countries who also worked for the Occupation Forces. He would come to my office on business three or four times a week. Often we both had to go to the Sanssouci Palace in Potsdam, which was the Russian Komandantura. I was always disgusted when I went there. The Sanssouci had been a beautiful palace—and is again today—but during the Russian occupation it was a pig sty. The Russians would wipe their boots off with the gorgeous drapes and then sit with their boots propped up on once beautiful desks, digging deep gouges in them. They smoked a terrible, cheap tobacco called *majorka* wrapped in newspaper, and they reeked of nicotine and alcohol.

On this particular occasion I was sitting in an outer office at the Sanssouci waiting to see one of these Russians, and I heard terrible shouting and cursing coming from his office. Shortly, my doctor friend rushed out. He was flushed and obviously very upset. He went straight out the door and did not even say hello to me. Since Russians were always screaming at people, I did not think too much about it.

CROSSING THE ELDE BRIDGE

A few days later I was in my office in Berlin with my secretary, Lilo. I was very fortunate to have a secretary. She was a typical Berliner, sassy, very competent, and knew the city well. Although she was quite a bit older than I, we soon became good friends. I remarked that I had not seen the doctor, which was odd, because he always came around several times a week.

"Oh, haven't you heard?" Lilo asked.

"About the doctor? What?" I had not told her what I had heard in the Russian's office a few days earlier.

"Oh, my God. He died."

"He what?" I was shocked.

"Yes, he caught a terrible case of the flu and died three days ago."

I was stunned. He had died the day after he had rushed out of the Russian's office. I had no doubt that the officer had either killed him or had him killed over whatever they were arguing about.

My job required that I go to many social functions put on by the Russians. They seemed to live on vodka. I hated it, but at those parties I had to drink with them. As often as I could I would find some place to pour out my drink and fill my glass with water. Still, I had to be careful and pace myself. Parties didn't end until everyone was drunk.

On one occasion the Russian officers had brought their wives. One wife appeared dressed in a beautiful blue—nightgown. She wore the nightgown with boots, and she had pinned paper flowers in her hair. At a formal occasion in Berlin. She was showing off her best.

❧

BACK TO BERLIN

Two KGB officers often came to my office on business also. The KGB wore green hats, and when I saw those green hats coming, I wanted to vomit. I had to be business-like and dignified, but when they appeared I always died inside from repulsion. Even today it makes my stomach turn to think about the KGB.

Eventually, one of the KGB officers began visiting daily, bringing me gifts, such as a slab of bacon wrapped in newspaper. That was very valuable, like a gift of dozen roses, but it made me ill. He called me Rosa because I was "beautiful like a rose." He would say to Lilo in his broken German, "She Rosa. She beautiful. She like a rose. I rich man. I live Omsk. I big house. Grandmother, mother, wife, cow, goat, chickens all live in house. I take Rosa to Omsk. Make wife."

And Lilo would ask, "How are you going to make her your wife? You have a wife in Omsk."

"Omsk wife old. I kick out. Rosa new wife."

When Lilo told me this, I sat there quaking in fear, because the KGB officer had the power to do just that.

At first, I only had to put up with this awful man in the office, but after a while he started following me home. By this time the *Ubahn* and *Esbahn* had started running, and I would take one or the other to get home. To my horror one evening I climbed onto to *Esbahn*, and there was the green hat. I ignored him, and when I got to my stop I raced home. The next night I took the *Ubahn* instead, and there he was again. I knew I had to get away from Berlin or I would end up scrubbing floors and rearing Russian children in Omsk. But I also knew couldn't continue searching for my parents, my grandmother, and my husband if I left, so I decided to remain and take my chances.

19

Wittenberge

One summer day a friend in the Red Cross called me. "Maria, I have good news. I have just received a report that your father is in Wittenberge." I was overjoyed to hear that Tata was alive. I sobbed with relief. Wittenberge was only about eighty miles away, and I got permission to go see him.

I arrived in Wittenberge and found his apartment building. It was one of those typical, old European tenements. From the street you see one big entrance and then you walk into a large courtyard surrounded by apartments. From that courtyard you walk into another and maybe even a third, and in each one there are apartments all the way around. It was really horrible, but in those times, if something was not destroyed by bombs, it was precious. If you could get a bed to sleep somewhere and it did not rain on you or the wind did not blow through broken windows, you were very fortunate. This was a luxury. No heat, but you had a roof over your head.

Tata's address was on the third floor in a tiny room in the

apartment of a rather unsavory woman, Minna Mueller, one of those people who has a good heart but not very high morals. When Minna answered the door, I introduced myself and I asked about my father.

"Oh, he'll be along shortly. He's very punctual. You know, he's a good looking man but such a big fool. I tried and tried as hard as I could to get him in my bed, but he never would. No, he's such a fool."

She chatted on, "He is mourning your mother; he doesn't know if she's alive or dead. He thinks she's probably dead. And he doesn't know if you are alive or not. I've been afraid for him. He's so depressed and sad, like he's just waiting, even wanting, to die. He's withering away." This would have been my parents' twenty-fifth wedding anniversary, so I could only imagine how he must have felt.

When she stopped to take a breath, I asked, "Where is he now?"

"Oh, he's working in a factory. He should be home in twenty minutes or so."

She continued gabbing. "You know, I'm a good-looking woman, aren't I? And I'm clean. I'm clean, you know. I always make sure I clean up afterward." I didn't have the luxury of telling her to be quiet, because I was in her home. I had not seen my father in three years, so I listened, grateful for anything I could learn about Tata.

She was looking out the window. "Here he comes."

I ran over to see him down in the courtyard. The last time I had seen my father he was tall and handsome with black hair. He had always been very athletic, very fit. He sailed, climbed mountains. What I saw down in that courtyard was a stooped, white-haired man with sunken cheeks and hollow eyes. I gasped, "Oh, my God." I was glad Minna had told me he was in such bad shape, and that I was able to see him before he came to the door, so that I was prepared for his appearance.

I had a few minutes to pull myself together as we listened to him ponderously ascend the stairs. In a panic, I told Minna to say something to him before he saw me, so that he would not be too shocked. I stepped behind the door.

She opened it and stepped out into the hall. "You have a visitor, a young woman. She came to see you especially."

I coughed and slipped out from behind the door. For a moment Tata and I stood there staring at each other. He looked so dejected, so changed. And I was changed, too, no longer the teenager he had known. Then we melted into each other's arms. We sat on the sofa, holding each other's hands, both talking at once. Minna went into her kitchen and made us some tea, then had the decency to leave us alone.

Tata had indeed contemplated suicide, but as we sat there talking, his soul seemed to return and he appeared younger and younger as the minutes passed. I wanted to know everything about him. What had happened to him? How had he been separated from my mother and grandmother? So many questions I had. In some ways he had suffered more than I had.

He, Mamá, and Oma had stayed in Berlin all during the bombing. At the time he was still traveling to Potsdam. On his return from one such trip, before the collapse of the Eastern Front, he discovered that Mamá and Oma had been taken away by the Nazis. He was devastated, but there was nothing he could do. He roamed the city just trying to survive like so many others.

Once he had been accosted by three Russian soldiers and made the same mistake I did in Eldena. When these three stopped Tata and started yelling at him, my father was so frightened he thought he would ingratiate himself to them by speaking Croatian. As soon as he said something, they were enraged. "*Ti špion! Ti špion!* Spy! Spy!" They beat him and, pointing their weapons at him, ordered him to undress. He supposed they were going to shoot him right there and did not want to damage his clothes. The Russian troops were so poorly clothed that in many instances they had cardboard tied around their feet, because their boots had worn out. They had nothing, so they stole.

As Tata undressed, he dropped his coat here, his pants there, shoes and socks, everything he had to take off until he stood stark naked amidst the rubble, surrounded by these three Russians who were about to shoot him. But then they started to argue. "I want the pants." "No, I want the pants." My father saw a basement entrance in the ruins of an adjacent building. While the Russians argued over his clothes, he raced naked and barefoot through the debris to the basement and bounded down the stairs into a crowd of women, old men, and children. They were not particularly surprised by his nakedness. He asked for clothes and they came up with enough to cover him. He waited a while, then ventured back out. The Russians were gone, and so were his clothes.

That is when he decided to leave Berlin and make his way to Laaslich. The house there was full with Tante Grete, Mariechen, Grandmother, Erwin, and several cousins. Uncle Otto had been taken away by then. Father was useful; he could fix anything. He repaired as much of the remaining farm equipment as he could, but he knew he could not stay long. There was very little to eat and so many mouths. After a week he left and made his way to Wittenberge.

He found a job working for the Russians in an old Singer Sewing Machine factory. They were dismantling everything. They even broke open the walls to take out the pipes and wire. Then it was all loaded onto flatcars to be shipped back to the Soviet Union. But the trains never went anywhere. It snowed and thawed and rained. The cars just sat there and all those pipes loaded on them rusted and deteriorated to uselessness, because the Russians were so disorganized. This job was far beneath my father, but in these times a university degree meant nothing. If you had an opportunity to get money to buy food, you did whatever you had to do.

⌘

As Tata talked I could see that I would have to be careful what I told him about my own experiences. I was very close to him, and I wanted to unburden myself, but I noticed that when I told him some of the things that had happened to me, not even the worst, he became furious.

I did not want him to do anything foolish. Where he worked soldiers were constantly watching. He was not an aggressive man, but he had a sense of fairness and could become agitated over things that upset him. I could see that just a spark would make him explode. He could have done something or said something to a Russian, and that would have been it. So, I told him very little of my life in the past few years.

Because I had a bad feeling about his work situation, I decided that I had to get him out of Wittenberge. First, though, I did have good news for him. Right before I had left for Wittenberge, I had found out that my mother and grandmother were still alive.

After my return to Berlin, I had learned that the Nazis had made good their threat of deporting my mother and grandmother; they had sent them to a work camp in Czechoslovakia which the Russians took over when the Eastern Front collapsed. Now I had discovered through the Red Cross that they were going to be shipped east, which meant only one thing: we would never see them again. So I was trying to arrange their return to western Germany to a refugee camp in Sinsheim south of Heidelberg. When I told Tata, he was beside himself with joy.

I needed to get him out of Wittenberge, make sure my mother and grandmother got safely to the American area and somehow reunited with my father, and also get myself out of Berlin. But first I had to return to Berlin, and my mind was in a frenzy trying to determine out how all these things could be done.

20
Reunited

My most immediate concern when I returned to Berlin at week's end was to make sure Mamá and Oma had, in fact, started back to Germany. As I learned later, while still in Berlin my mother had been forced to wash tanks for the Russians. Apparently, the Russian officer in charge was not satisfied with her work, and for no other reason, planned to ship her and my grandmother east to God knows where. When I discovered that they were in the camp in Czechoslovakia and scheduled to be deported farther east, I forged birth certificates to show both had been born in Germany and submitted these to the Red Cross to get them reclassified as German refugees. I thought maybe there is a God, because I learned on my return to Berlin after visiting my father that they were at that moment in a group of refugees headed for Sinsheim.

I also knew in my heart that as soon as they could, my mother and grandmother would want to go to Berlin to look for my father and me, since that was the last place they knew he had been.

CROSSING THE ELDE BRIDGE

I had to get to them and keep that from happening, since I had heard pretty reliable rumors that Berlin, like the rest of Germany was to be divided into sectors, each to be administered by one of the Occupation Forces. I did not want Mamá and Oma to end up in the Russian sector, so as soon as I could a few weeks later, I forged travel documents and made my way to Sinsheim.

Travel was severely restricted. Fortunately, part of my job was to issue traveling passes to those who were entitled to them, so it was easy to forge an *interzonenpass*, but the Russians were always very suspicious and often refused to honor any kind of documentation. On this particular trip I was so frightened that as soon as the train started moving and before the military conductors came around to inspect our papers, I locked myself in the toilet and hoped the guards would not break down the door. When the train stopped at the border between the Russian and American areas, I jumped off and raced into the forest. The border was not fenced and mined yet, but it was heavily guarded, at least on the Russian side. I moved quietly forward, often stopping and crouching down, until I got to the cleared strip which was the actual border.

Off to my right not far away a group of soldiers sat around a little fire. They appeared to be playing cards and by their loud talk and cursing, I knew they were drunk. I was not much worried about them. But two other guards walked back and forth in the clearing. These two were dangerous. If they saw me, I knew what they would do, and I suppose they had some legal right to shoot me. So I crouched there in the bushes waiting and watching like a hunted animal until I saw my chance. Both guards were walking away from me, and I jumped up and rushed across the border. I did not look back to see if they saw or heard me, but they did not fire. Again luck.

Once into the woods on the American side I walked quickly back to the train tracks, expecting to catch the next train, but my luck was still good. The train I had been on was just beginning to move away from the Russian checkpoint, so I leaped on it when it stopped to pick up the American guards and went on my way. The Americans who boarded checked my pass, but there wasn't any problem.

In the early morning I finally arrived at Sinsheim, an ugly, gray town, and found the camp. I think it might have been a concentration camp during the war. It looked like one, rows and rows of austere barracks surrounded by an imposing wire fence. I found the camp director's office and was guided to the barracks where my mother and grandmother were located. I took a deep breath, and stepped inside. Two tiers of raised sleeping platforms ran down either side of the long, almost windowless building. Each individual had a straw mattress. I walked in and I saw two totally emaciated figures in robes. My God, it was Mamá and Oma.

They did not see me at first and I had to stand there for a while and compose myself. I did not want them to see me crying. I wanted to be positive. I was disheveled from crawling through the woods at the border but otherwise looked healthy, since I had lived in Berlin for a while. And all that bacon from the KGB officer. I wasn't even hungry anymore.

I straightened myself, smiled, and started walking towards them. My grandmother and my poor mother saw me and were stunned.

We rushed into each other's arms, the three of us clutching each other and wailing. We were swaying back and forth, clinging to each other. Just to hold these two frail bodies overwhelmed me. We could not speak, only cry and hold tightly to one another in a dance of joy.

They were astonished that I was there. They had no idea, no idea why they were brought back to Germany and no idea where they were going. I had brought some food with me which I gave to them, and then we talked and talked. I told them what I had been doing and that I had been able to pull a few strings to get them relocated.

The first thing they mentioned was that they wanted to get to Berlin to look for my father. I told them absolutely not. "First of all," I said, "Berlin is totally destroyed, and secondly, there are going to be changes in Berlin that I cannot talk about, but you can't come back. You have to stay here." And I told them I had to get out of Berlin myself, because of the Umsk Russian. I told them all about him.

With a big smile I said, "And besides, Tata isn't in Berlin. He's in Wittenberge—and I'm bringing him here." At that point I did not know how I was going to do it, but I knew I had to get my father out of Wittenberge, and since he couldn't go to Berlin, I thought I might as well try to bring him to Sinsheim.

I stayed in Sinsheim several days, and we talked endlessly. Both Mamá and Oma had had a rough time. Neither had been raped, but both had been horribly mistreated and abused. A young Russian soldier had asked my grandmother for a ring she was wearing. One did not say no to the Russians. If they wanted your earrings, for instance, and you were not fast enough taking them off, they just ripped them out of your ears or cut your ears off. But Oma said no, and he slapped her across the face, a tiny seventy-year-old woman. My grandmother looked up at him and slapped him right back. He was stunned. Then she said to him,

"Shame on you. I could be your *babushka*, your grandmother. Is that how they taught you to treat your *babushka*?" Amazingly, the young Russian apologized.

Oma was in fairly good health, but Mamá was extremely ill. She told me that in prison in Czechoslovakia she had terrible hemorrhages and was seen by a doctor there, another prisoner. He informed her that she had a tangerine-sized tumor in her uterus and should have surgery immediately. Of course, that was out of the question.

When my mother told me about her condition, I started thinking. Perhaps I could bring Roland as well as my father here, and we could all be together. So after the reunion with my mother and grandmother, I returned to Berlin and started making arrangements.

♾

Again, I had to forge passes for Tata and me and get us from Wittenberge to Berlin to the boundary of the Russian zone. My father was a rather proud man to be told what to do by his daughter. But I was the one who had already crossed over and knew what was involved, so he followed my instructions, and we got past the Russian checkpoint without incident. I put him on the train headed for Sinsheim and took myself back to Berlin. I only wish I could have been there when my parents and my grandmother were reunited in Sinsheim.

My father was not part of that refugee group and so was not allowed to remain in Sinsheim. But he had had a brother who had died a number of years before, my godfather, Uncle Paul, who had lived in Prague and also had owned a villa in Schliersee. Schliersee is in the Alps and has always been known as a spa because of its natural springs and its beauty. The town is on a lake with a little island in the center, and it is surrounded by mountains. Because his brother had owned the villa in Schliersee, Tata was allowed to go there.

A short time later, I returned to Sinsheim. I was happy to hear that my parents and grandmother had been reunited before Tata was sent to Schliersee. Mamá also told me that the camp director seemed to be very empathetic. She was extremely weak, but she said, "Let's go with Oma and talk to him."

I introduced myself as the daughter and granddaughter of these two ladies, and I asked the camp director point blank how many refugees were in his group. He told me 614. Looking him straight in the eye, I asked, "Are you sure there're not 616?" Then I explained my situation to him, about the KGB officer and my child. I could not stay in Laaslich, because my Russian admirer could easily have found me there. Besides, the rest of my family were all in the south, except for my husband, and I had no idea where he might be. I hadn't heard a word in years. And the camp director, God bless him, said, "Well, of course. Didn't I say 616?" And so I became a member of that camp.

∽᳁∾

Now there only remained for me to retrieve Roland and get away from Berlin. I was not going to leave the Russian area without my child. Nobody in Berlin could know of my departure, so I returned there secretly, collected up a few things, and went straight to Laaslich to get Roland. From there I fled south again, sneaked across the border, and made my way to Sinsheim.

We did not stay in the camp very long. It was actually a clearing house for refugees. As accommodations became available, people from the camp were assigned to them wherever they happened to be. My mother and grandmother went to live there in Sinsheim. They had one small room in a house owned by an old woman. Locals across Germany generally disliked refugees, because we were such a burden. Roland and I were sent to live in a dentist's house in Adelsheim about thirty miles away, and Tata stayed on in Uncle Paul's villa in Schliersee.

These were not the best arrangements, but we were all safe. My only hope now was that my husband was alive and would return from God knows where, so we could be a family again.

21
Tragedy

Adelsheim was a nightmare. I do not even remember how many families lived in the house we were assigned to. Again, I was given a tiny room barely able to accommodate a small bed, a table with two chairs, and a little stove not as big as a TV set. A rope was strung from one corner to the other to hang things on, not that I had much to hang. That is where I spent the winter with Roland—and everybody in the house hated us, because poor Roland was crying constantly. How would you feel if two or three families with squalling children moved into your house? Roland slept very little and only for short periods, and then he would stand on the bed and scream his heart out.

After my months in Berlin where I ate well, I was starving again. So was everyone. There was not enough food to go around. Worse, the house had one small kitchen, which we all had to share. Gas was turned on only during certain hours, so we were all assigned specific times to use the stove. If I had a potato or something to boil, I had to wait my turn. And then, if Roland needed attending and I had to leave the kitchen, my potato would be gone when I came back.

For people who have never lived in extreme conditions like that, it is impossible to understand what happens to human beings. Perfectly normal individuals who are otherwise honorable and decent become different. When you are cold and hungry, you will do whatever you can to survive. Not only would people steal my food from the kitchen, the owners of the house often would not even let me into the kitchen. If I had something to heat up, a little milk or water, whatever I had, the owner's wife often would tell me to get out. I would say, "But my boy is hungry." And she would reply, "It will make no difference, he's going to cry anyway."

An American camp was nearby, and every afternoon I would bundle up Roland and go there. The staff who ran the commissary would dump leftover food into a pit and leave for a while before coming back to pour gasoline in and burn everything. In the meantime, a group of half-starved people which I was part of would appear, and we would throw ourselves on those scraps like animals. I remember grabbing a half-eaten pork chop, a chicken bone with a small scrap of meat on it, a piece of bread, whatever I could get my hands on. Surviving was not easy.

Among our group were nuns who had a little pull cart much like the one which I had had when I left Eldena. The Americans often threw away large amounts of rotten vegetables. The nuns would always go for the onions and fill their cart. One day I asked a nun why. "Well," she explained, "They are rotten on the outside, but inside there is a core that's not rotten and onions have a great amount of vitamin C. We have an orphanage with so many little children who desperately need vitamin C. Of course, we could use other food too, but we can't take it all, so that's why we take the onions."

Hunger was not our only problem. It was frigid, and there was almost no wood or coal to heat with. I used the little stove in my room as often as I could find fuel. The owners of the house would not give me any wood, and since there was a lumber mill not far away, I went there with a bag to gather a few wood scraps or even sawdust. A guard saw me once and started yelling, "Get out of here, you goddamn whore!" He was going to shoot me for trying to take a few pieces of scrap wood. Even those were passed to someone else for money or favors, and I had nothing to trade, so I didn't get any. I often went around breaking off branches of bushes to use for fuel, but even that was stealing.

During that winter I began helping a Catholic priest. He was ministering to seventeen surrounding communities, and all he had to get around on was a bicycle. He had almost no resources and many desperate refugees to take care of. I assisted him in every way I could, helping him get food and clothing for people. Twice we received a care package from the Americans, and I helped him distribute the items inside. I remember sitting at his table with a large can of powdered eggs. We had so many families who had children who needed those eggs. We made small strips of powder on the table and divided them up as best we could. I could easily have taken one or more of them, but I couldn't do it. As needy as we were, there were others who were worse off, who didn't even have a roof over their heads.

Through the priest, I met a doctor, also a refugee, who examined Roland. I was really concerned about him. After the doctor had looked him over and spent some time watching him, he told me what I did not want to hear. He said that Roland had been so traumatized, physically and emotionally, he probably would not live to adulthood, and the best I could expect was that he would be severely retarded. The most I could hope for was that he might be able to be a goatherd or to do some other menial task.

◦◦

Again I was totally depressed. Again I was at the end of my rope. Friendless, freezing, hungry, trying to support and nurture a child who was probably not going to live, my parents and everyone who loved me far away. And then, a final blow. The government notified me that Jurgen had died in a Russian prison camp. I was a widow.

And into this bottomless pit, this blackness, a guardian angel appeared. My father, again full of strength and self-confidence, came to Adelsheim. I was overjoyed to see him.

As I have said, he was sent to Schliersee and obtained a room in his brother's old villa. Many people already lived there, even though it had sustained considerable damage, not from bombs but from vandalism. An SS training school had been located nearby, and I think the villa might have been used as a barracks by the SS during the war.

After the war, the country was filled with hate and discontent. The Jews still alive hated the Germans. Many Germans hated the Jews, especially those who operated the black market and were getting rich from it. Everybody hated the Russians who hated everybody in return. Perhaps this hatred was understandable, but it did not help matters.

Because of this situation, the villa had been vandalized. There was no heat. Most of the windows were broken. Doors had been torn down and used for fuel. My father would leave a glass of water on his table at night, and in the morning it would be ice.

When Tata had arrived in Schliersee, he was desperate for a job, anything. There was no industry in Schliersee, only hotels and spas, most of which were still closed, but in Hausham, five miles away, there was a coal mine, and he went there to find work. Later, fortunately, he found a job repaving the streets. At first it was terrible for him. He had to walk the five miles from Schliersee to Hausham in the cold, work outside all day, and return again on foot to a frigid room. And, like us in Adelsheim, everyone in Schliersee was half-starved also. A baker near Tata's work site gave him stale buns, and that was often all he had to eat.

Life got better for him. He eventually brought my mother and grandmother to Schliersee, and they had two rooms in a typical Bavarian house. And he also obtained a bicycle. That bike probably meant more to him than any of the many automobiles he had owned ever did.

Until he came to Adelsheim my father had no idea how miserably I lived. After I told him about Roland's diagnosis and Jurgen's death, my wonderful father said, "This is not going to continue. You two cannot suffer like this." And he took Roland back with him to Schliersee. I cried when they left, but I knew life there would be better for my child. Besides, things would improve and we would be together again. I knew it.

❧❧

The following summer I got permission to visit Schliersee. The house where my parents and grandmother lived was lovely, filled with hand-carved furniture, and Frau Newmann, the owner, was a very compassionate and caring woman. My parents had a large, sunny room on the third floor that was reached by climbing outside stairs to a sunny patio with flowers and vegetables in pots and even a chicken coop with a few chickens. Roland weakly clung to my father and mother and was shy around me, which broke my heart but was fortunate, because I knew I could not take him back to Adelsheim.

Food restrictions were worse than during the war, and with a traumatized child and a sick wife—my mother was suffering terribly from her cancer—my father had difficulty feeding everyone. Frau Newmann, who had a cow in addition to the chickens and garden, often gave them milk, eggs, and vegetables out of the kindness of her heart, but it was still an effort to get enough food.

I think that was part of the reason that my parents and Jurgen's parents decided to move Roland to Laaslich shortly after I returned to Adelsheim. For one thing, the Kohlers had more food on the farm, and Roland would be better fed. He would also be in the fresh air and sunshine. Perhaps a little later in his life, he could help herd the goats and sheep—if he lived. My father didn't write to me that he was taking Roland to Laaslich until he had returned to Schliersee. I was upset when I heard what the four grandparents had done, but in my heart knew it was for the best. I would have difficulty seeing Roland again because of the travel restrictions in the Russian area, but I knew he would have a better life in Laaslich.

The following fall I received another letter from my father. I excitedly opened it, only to collapse in a chair. I reread my father's devastating news. Roland, my poor, darling Roland, whom I had carried on my back all those months and all those miles, had finally succumbed to the years of starvation and trauma. My Roland was dead.

I was numb. I had lost my child and my husband. I was widowed, destitute, and probably emotionally scarred for life. I can't go on I thought. I cannot take any more. Then I thought of Oma and what she taught me. "Don't ever think the word 'can't.' 'Cannot' does not exist in your vocabulary." I vowed that somehow I would continue to survive.

22
Crossing the Elde Bridge

Two years later I remarried and moved to Mexico, where I lived for several years before eventually coming to the United States. My mother died in 1952, and my father married my stepmother, Hanne, a few years later. Tata, Hanne, and Oma lived together in Schliersee, and I visited often. Hanne and I grew very close, and I continued my yearly visits, even after Tata and Oma had passed away. But I had lost track of Jurgen's family, because they were living in what had become East Germany behind the Iron Curtain. I had no idea whether any of them were still alive or where they might be.

In the Spring of 1991, after the Berlin Wall had come down and the Iron Curtain had disintegrated, I was sitting on my front porch enjoying the warm sunshine, watching the ducks in the lake across the street, and waving to the occasional passerby when the phone rang. I didn't have a cordless phone or an answering machine at the time and was too comfortable to go inside to answer, so I just let it ring. Finally it stopped.

Five minutes later it rang again, this time with what I imagined a greater urgency. I finally got up, went inside, and picked up the phone.

"Hello."

"*Guten Tag.* Good afternoon. Is this Mrs. Clark?" A German voice, a male. For many years I had been a volunteer with the American Field Service, an international student exchange program, so at first I thought it might be one of my old exchange students. But I was puzzled. Anyone who would speak German to me would be someone whom I knew and who knew me. Why was this man asking if I were Mrs. Clark? Then I was alarmed.

"Who is this?" I asked in German.

"Mrs. Clark, my name is Roland Kohler, and I believe I am your son."

I sank into the armchair next to the phone, unable to speak.

"Mrs. Clark? Mrs. Clark?"

"Yes, I'm here," I replied in a weak voice. "I...I don't think you could possibly be my son. He died many years ago when he was a small child."

"Well, Mrs. Clark, I don't know exactly what happened, but I can assure you that I am Roland Kohler, and I'm very much alive." He mentioned that he was calling from Schliersee. Then he asked if I knew Breitestrasse, the street my husband's parents lived on in Berlin where I had first lived as a young bride. He also asked if I knew Laaslich.

"No! No!" I retorted, adrenalin pounding through my veins. I was hyperventilating. Was this man KGB? Had the Russians found me? Visions flooded my mind. I was being beaten to death.

I was being shot. I was being raped. Finally, I collected myself enough to say, "Look, why don't you write me a long letter about all of this. Then maybe we can talk, but I can tell you now that I'm not your mother." Shaking, I quickly hung up.

Then I totally panicked and began pacing around the house. I had to leave. I had to get away, but where could I go? Mexico? Costa Rica? I had friends in both places. But if I went, would the Russians find me again? Then I stopped. I told myself I was being unrealistic and I tried to think more rationally, only to have another panic attack. I was hysterical, a mad woman.

At that moment the doorbell rang. I stood there, hardly able to breath. Okay, Maria, calm yourself. Settle down. Stop this. I straightened myself, walked slowly to door, unlocked it. There stood my neighbor, George. His parents and I had been friends for many years, and I had known George as a boy and now as a young man.

Eyebrows raised, he looked at me. "What's wrong with you?"

I quickly pulled him through the entry, slamming the door shut and locking it behind him.

"What do you mean, what's wrong with me?" I shrieked.

He ignored my hysterics. "Listen to you. Look at yourself. You're pale as a ghost, and you're screaming."

"Something terrible has happened, but I can't talk about it right now," and then I began to cry.

George comforted me and patted my arm. "Listen, whatever it is, you need to calm down. Let me take you to a movie and dinner. Come on."

The last thing I wanted to do was go to a movie, but I allowed him to usher me out the door, and I must say that the next few hours away helped even though I didn't pay much attention to the film.

I was exhausted when I got home but unable to sleep. I didn't even try to go to bed. I paced most of the night, trying to think what to do. The next day I was to meet my friends, the Newmans, for lunch with several others. Marvin and Myrna Newman had been close friends for many years. Under the circumstances I thought I would have to cancel with them, but toward morning, I decided that I would discuss the situation with Marvin. I finally lay down for a few hours of fitful sleep.

I awoke in plenty of time to bathe, dress, and drive off to meet the Newmans at a local restaurant. After we were settled, I whispered to Marvin that I needed to speak to him privately. We excused ourselves and went outside. I trusted Marvin implicitly. He was not only my close friend, but also a successful lawyer and college professor and a very wise man. I told him what had happened.

"First of all," he said, "you have nothing to fear. You are being unrealistic about the KGB. Those days are over. No one is tracking you down. Secondly, this may be the best thing that has happened to you in your life, ever. You have to contact this man and find out more. Do you know how to reach him?"

I did not, but this Roland, or whoever he was, had told me he was calling from a hotel in Schliersee. My stepmother, Hanne, and my friends, the Scharnagels, who lived next door to her, were all in Schliersee, so I decided to seek their help in locating this man.

When I arrived home, I called Hanne first. Yes, a nicely dressed middle-aged man with a teenager and little boy had come to her door. The Scharnagels and I both had told Hanne over and over again not to answer the door unless she knew the person ringing the bell. She was able to view the entrance to the building from her bathroom window and didn't recognize the man or the boys, so she didn't go to the door. Finally, the group walked away.

Then I called the Scharnagels and spoke to their daughter, Irene. This man had also visited her. He was well-dressed and articulate, and the boys were quiet and well-mannered, so Irene invited them in. Roland told her his story and was passionate and sincere. He even showed her his birth certificate. Irene thought he might be my son, so she gave him my address and phone number. "I am sorry, Maria. I asked him to please write to you first because of your bad heart. I guess I shouldn't have given him your phone number."

"It's not a problem, Irene. I was just startled by his phone call. I'm still not sure he is my son, but from what you've told me, it sounds as if he might be. I can't believe he's alive, though. I need to talk to him. Did he tell you where he is staying?" He had, and Irene gave me the phone number of the Pension Schmidtbauer.

Finally, I phoned Marvin and told him what I had learned. Without hesitation, Marvin said, "Call him, Maria. Call him right now. I think he could very well be your son, so call him. You won't regret it."

After I'd hung up the phone, I sat there, thinking. Could this really be my son? Why had my parents told me he had died? Had they lied to me? And what about all the trauma Roland had suffered? How had he overcome that? From all I had learned so far, I knew there was a strong possibility that he was my son. And wouldn't it be wonderful if it were true? What a miracle to have him back!

Shaking, I picked up the phone, dialed the Pension

CROSSING THE ELDE BRIDGE

Schmidtbauer in Schliersee and asked for Roland Kohler.

"*Hallo! Guten Tag!*"

I hesitated for some seconds then responded. "Roland, this is Maria Clark. I believe you may be correct. I think I am your mother." I heard him gasp, and I could tell he was crying. I was too. We talked for a long time.

⁓ා ෴

Roland related that he had been told I was dead, but he had always had nagging uncertainties. He had no memory of me, but he did have vague memories of a tall, dark-haired, pretty lady (my mother) holding his hand and walking to a lake with him. He even had a dim memory of falling into a chicken coop. And he knew that his maternal grandparents lived, or had lived, in Schliersee, which was in West Germany. From the time he was a youngster, he had decided that if ever he could, he would go to Schliersee to find out about his grandparents. After the fall of the Iron Curtain, he got the chance and took his wife and two of his three children to look for his maternal grandparents and perhaps even his mother.

He went first to the Catholic Church in Schliersee and learned that his grandparents had lived there, but both were dead. He also learned that his grandfather had survived his grandmother and had remarried. His widow was still alive. He took his two sons, one a teenager and the other a small boy, to Hanne's house and rang the bell. No one answered. He rang again and waited. There was no response.

As they were leaving Roland saw a group of older people sitting on benches in front of the apartment building next door, so he approached them. "Good afternoon," he said. "I'm looking for someone, a woman in her mid-sixties, who may be related to the lady next door."

They all looked at him, smiling and nodding. These people had seen me year after year and knew that I was from America. One of them was also the local postman and had delivered my frequent letters to Hanne and the Scharnagels.

"Yes, yes. You're right," said the postman. "There is a lady who comes every summer, and, yes, she was our neighbor's daughter. He's dead now, but the stepmother lives right there. She's a nice lady, says hello but never tells us anything. I do know from delivering the mail that the woman, the visitor, lives in Florida in America. You need to go over to the Scharnagels. They're good friends. I think the Scharnagels' daughter has even visited her in Florida."

Roland and the two boys headed over to the house the group had pointed out. When he rang the door bell, Irene Scharnagel answered. He introduced himself and his children and gave her his card. Irene invited them into the house. Roland then proceeded to tell her his history; he even showed her his personal identification, including his birth certificate from the hospital in Wittenberge, which had miraculously survived all those years. Irene finally gave him my address and phone number, and admonished him to write first.

Leaving the Scharnagels, he raced back to the hotel and burst into the room where his family was staying, so excited he could hardly control himself. His wife, Doris, was enjoying a nice, hot bath and a book. "Doris, Doris, I found her! I found her!"

Doris had always thought that her mother-in-law was long dead, and she was absorbed in her book and her bath. "Yeah, yeah. Close the door. You're letting the cold air in."

"No, Doris. I really have found her!" He paced back and forth. "I've got to call her. I've just got to call her." Roland knew he had promised Irene to write first, but he was overwhelmed by his own enthusiasm.

Exasperated, Doris finally said, "Okay, go ahead and call her. Just leave me in peace." She knew this woman wasn't Roland's mother. Roland raced downstairs to the lobby and called the woman he thought was his mother on the only phone in the hotel.

At the end of our conversation, Roland agreed to write to me as soon as he returned home. As I hung up I thought how thankful I was that Marvin had convinced me to call back.

❧❧

I began to believe that Roland was my son and wanted to visit him and his family. I called Marvin to get his opinion. Marvin suggested, instead, that Roland should come alone to visit me first. He thought it would be better for me to meet Roland on my home ground. Going back to Berlin, Laaslich, and that entire area was going to be traumatic for me.

When Roland and I next talked on the phone, I suggested that he visit. The conversation was awkward. I didn't know this man, and I tended to think of people from places like the GDR (East Germany) at that time as backward and unsophisticated. When he made some comment about flying "over the big pond," I thought he might never have been on an airplane and was afraid of flying, so I told him, "Oh, don't worry. Flying is very safe."

"I know that! I fly all over," he curtly replied.

"Oh," I said in a small voice. "Well, then, it's no problem. And I don't suppose you'll have any problem getting off work, when your boss understands the situation."

He interrupted me, "I am the boss. I'm the regional manager for the State's supermarket system and the nursing homes. I decide who goes and who does not."

Again, I could only answer, "Oh." This is a great way to start our reunion, I thought. Here I've put my foot in my mouth twice. He must take me for an idiot.

"Do you really want me to come?" he asked in a more gentle voice.

"Yes, yes I do."

"You're sure."

"Yes, I'm sure."

"Okay. I'll call you back."

We hung up. In a few months, I was going to see my son, my son whom I had carried all over Germany during those horrific months, my son who had been so traumatized, my son who had been dead. I began thinking about all I had to do around the house—repairs, a good cleaning, sprucing up the yard—as well as planning meals and what we would do. Even three months seemed too short a time to prepare.

The very next day the phone rang. It was Roland. "I'm in a hurry, but I need to know. Do you really want me to come?"

"Of course, I do. Yes."

"Okay, I can come for a week. I'll be there next Monday."

My heart leaped into my throat. "Wonderful," I said, but inside I thought, next Monday, oh my God. How will I ever get ready? On the one hand, it was wonderful. On the other hand, he was coming to visit in a few days. He was going to be here in this house. What would we say? What would we do? What if this was all a ruse? My mind was racing.

CROSSING THE ELDE BRIDGE

The day finally arrived and I went with two close friends to pick up Roland. I was afraid to go alone. In fact, I begged my friends to stay with me the whole time, but when we got to the airport, there were difficulties. The Gulf War was in full swing. No one was allowed to go to the gates. I explained my situation to the security people, and they very kindly escorted me. I was petrified.

Finally, after a few frightening moments of walking through the mostly deserted terminals, I was standing before the gate. Soon a jet rolled in and parked. People began disembarking up the ramp. I stood there with a pounding heart and sweating palms, in my hand a picture of Roland which he had mailed me. People continued to exit, but no Roland. Then a tall man wearing an Italian raincoat and carrying a leather brief case appeared. I didn't need a picture; he looked so much like his father. He was my son.

Our week together was glorious. We talked endlessly, sometimes all night. I had told only my closest friends about Roland. I did not want anything to interfere with our time together. We did go to the beach, and one day, through connections, I was able to take him on a tour of a Publix distribution center and a supermarket. But other than that, we just stayed home and caught up on the past forty-five years.

A few months after that first visit, he returned with his wife and three children, and I was embraced by a loving family I didn't even know I had. Since then we have visited back and forth many times, and we talk at least weekly on the phone.

❦

During our many hours of talking together, Roland told me

all about his life. He had spent his early years with his father, who was not dead after all but had been imprisoned by the Russians and had returned to Germany long after the war. Roland had spent his teenage years on the farm in Laaslich and had been told, when he was old enough to understand, that I had died during the war, just as I had been told he had died. Neither one of us will ever know why my parents and my in-laws decided to do this. We can only surmise that they felt Roland would be a burden to me, and that in order for me to get on with my life, a clean break with the past had to be made. We will never know exactly, because those who made the decision are all dead.

I also told Roland what had happened to me and that I still had nightmares about Eldena and escaping across the bridge. I would wake up in the middle of the night screaming after all these years, because ghosts from the past were still hounding me. He took my hands and said, "When you come back to Germany, you and I will go to Eldena and cross that bridge together. This time I will hold you, and the ghosts will never come again."

The next year we did go back to Eldena, Roland and I. It had not changed very much. We stood in silence in the shade of the old chestnut tree by the bridge which crossed the Elde River and watched the water. In my mind I could see the bloated bodies— soldiers, young mothers, babies, one after the other floating down the river—and the cattle that had been shot and were rotting on the banks.

As I stood there recounting the horrors of those days to my son, an old couple passed by. The elderly man, who had a patch over one eye, stopped and introduced himself as Herr Schmidt. Because he didn't know us and we didn't appear to be from the area, he asked if he could help. Roland is so friendly and interested in other people, that he struck up a conversation with the man and began telling him my story. "Oh, my God, yes," Herr Schmidt nodded. "There's a large wood a few kilometers from here, and there was heavy fighting there, the last battle in this area, between an SS unit and the Russians."

And that is where I was, of course, with Roland. That is where I stuffed the pair of gloves into his mouth so he could not scream, because the Russians were shooting up into the trees at the SS troops. That's where the SS soldier died on top of me and where his blood soaked my back and trickled down onto Roland. And now all these years later I was standing by this infamous bridge where so many had perished and across which I had escaped death.

"I wasn't SS," he explained. "I had been shot in the eye on the Eastern Front and returned to Eldena. They didn't kill me, I guess, because they thought I was going to die anyway. Why waste a bullet?" And he began to tell us about the Russians' occupying the minister's house, about their raping and killing his wife, eighty-year-old mother, and nine-year-old daughter. He also told us that the minister had been thrown in prison and later beheaded. And he told us about the house's being turned into a prison, the prison where I had been held and from which I had escaped.

"Yes, I remember that," he said. "There was a young woman imprisoned in that house who somehow got away, and there was terrible trouble afterwards."

I thought, because of me more people were killed here. I saved Roland's life and my own, but who knows how many people were punished because I escaped? Yet how could I not be glad to have been spared when I thought of my son and his family cavorting

CROSSING THE ELDE BRIDGE

in my pool at home or romping in the grass. Had I not escaped that night, none of that ever would have been.

Finally, Mr. Schmidt and his wife went on their way. Roland looked at me and gave me an encouraging smile. Then he put his arm around my waist, and together we walked across the Elde Bridge in the bright sunshine.

Author's Note

Maria Clark and I have been neighbors and friends for over twenty years. She is in her eighties now, and she has not had an easy existence; her life in the years after World War II is a saga of struggles almost as painful as the years during the war. But in all the time I have known her, she has maintained a dignity, an inner strength that anyone can feel in her presence.

Today, she lives quietly and lectures as part of a Communications Ethics course on death and dying at a local college and at many churches, clubs, and schools. This book is an outgrowth of those lectures. She has dedicated her life to increasing awareness of the Holocaust and to breaking down the barriers of hatred and indifference among cultures. For many years she was active in the American Field Service, an international exchange program for high school students. She is adamantly opposed to war.

Because of her experiences she still retains a deathly fear of the Gestapo and especially the KGB, and in setting down her story we have changed the names of many of those individuals involved, not only to protect their privacy, but perhaps more importantly to give her peace of mind.

For health reasons Maria is no longer able to travel as frequently as she used to, but Roland and his family come to the United States at least once a year.

The events presented herein are as accurate as sixty-five-year old memories can be, and I have painstakingly avoided embellishing or misrepresenting them. I have visited many of the places mentioned, including Berlin and Laaslich. I also have talked to many of the people involved who are still alive. Roland Kohler is one of my dearest friends.

David Lapham

LaVergne, TN USA
20 May 2010
183441LV00003B/4/P